Collected
and Trans

ELAINE FEINSTEIN was born in Lanc... grew up in Leicester. She read English at Newnham College Cambridge. In 1980 she was made a Fellow of the Royal Society of Literature, and in 1990 she received a Cholmondeley Award. She also received an Honorary Doctorate from the University of Leicester. Carcanet publish her *Selected Poems*, *Daylight* (Poetry Book Society Recommendation), *Gold* and *After Pushkin*.

Also by Elaine Feinstein from Carcanet

Daylight
Gold
Selected Poems

ELAINE FEINSTEIN

*Collected Poems
and Translations*

CARCANET

First published in 2002 by
Carcanet Press Limited
4th Floor, Conavon Court
12–16 Blackfriars Street
Manchester M3 5BQ

A CIP catalogue record for this book
is available from the British Library

ISBN 1 85754 566 4 (trade paperback)
ISBN 1 85754 581 8 (library edition)
ISBN 1 85754 582 6 (limited edition)

The publisher acknowledges financial assistance
from the Arts Council of England

Set in Monotype Garamond by XL Publishing Services, Tiverton
Printed and bound in England by SRP Ltd, Exeter

Revival Books Ltd.

Unit 11 Hugh Business Park, Bacup Road
Waterfoot, Lancashire, BB4 7BT
United Kingdom
Books@RevivalBooks.co.uk
01706 227207
www.revivalbooks.co.uk

Contents

THE CELEBRANTS (1973)

SOME UNEASE AND ANGELS (1977)

BADLANDS (1986)

CITY MUSIC (1990)

SONGS FROM PLAYS

DAYLIGHT (1997)

GOLD (2000)

UNCOLLECTED POEMS

TRANSLATIONS

Translations from the Russian

Translation from the French

Translation from the German

Lyrics after Alexander Pushkin

Preface

People have always been the centre of my concerns, and as my poems usually spring from some experience in my own life, it is intimately disturbing to look back through more than three decades, and try to make out a line of development.

Part of my resistance to mainstream English poetry of the 1950s, when I first began to write, must lie in my own sense of being an outsider. Born in Liverpool into a family of Jewish immigrants from Odessa, and moreover a woman, it is hardly surprising that three privileged years at Newnham College, Cambridge were not enough to eradicate my sense of being at the periphery. In any case, I found the cautious, ironic tone of New Movement poetry, as it was then called, for the most part smugly insular. Nothing was more natural than for me to look across the Atlantic, to poets using English in a European modernist tradition. For a time, I was drawn to Black Mountain poets, particularly Charles Olson, and shared that enthusiasm with the followers of J.H. Prynne.

It was translation, however, that helped me to find my own voice and the great Russian poet Marina Tsvetaeva who proved to be the most important single influence on my poetry. The English poet and critic Donald Davie pointed out long ago that I recognised myself in her, even though my life was not marked by the tragedies of loss and exile that tormented hers. She was a dangerous example, since in both of us domestic impracticality meant the usual tensions of wife, mother and poet were written horrifyingly large. She taught me to be unafraid of exposing my least dignified emotions, as well as the technical discipline of a rhythm flowing down a page even when held in stanzas. After that, I rarely used completely open forms.

For many years I have worked most of all for directness and lucidity, because I distrust any music that drowns the pressure of what has been felt. Yet it is still the lyric I love. Wyatt at his most laconic, Herbert's simplicity, Pound's marvellous ear for syllables: these remain my models. And my central inspiration is probably best expressed by Joseph Brodsky, who wrote about imprisonment, exile and surgery – and could still feel gratitude for what Lawrence called the 'great privilege of being alive'.

ELAINE FEINSTEIN

In a Green Eye

Father

The wood trade in his hands
at sixtyone back at the sawbench,
my stubborn father sands and planes
birchwood for kitchen chairs.

All my childhood he was a rich man
unguarded purchaser
of salmon trout, off-season strawberries
and spring in Switzerland.

Bully to prudish aunts
whose niggard habits taught them to assess
honest advantage, without rhetoric:
his belly laughter overbore their tutting.

Still boss of his own shop
he labours in the chippings without grudge
loading the heavy tables,
shabby and powerful as an old bus.

Calliope in the Labour Ward

she who has no love for women
married and housekeeping

now the bird notes begin
in the blood in the June morning
look how these ladies are
as little squeamish as
men in a great war

have come into their bodies
as their brain dwindles to
the silver circle on
eyelids under sun
and time opens

pain in the shallows to wave up and over them

grunting in gas and air
they sail to a
darkness without self
where no will reaches

in that abandon less
than human
give birth
bleak as a goddess

Mother Love

You eat me, your
nights eat me
Once you took
haemoglobin and bone
out of my blood

Now my head
sleeps forward on my neck
holding you

In the morning my
skin shines hot
and you are happy
banging your fat hands,

I kiss your
soft feet mindless:
delicately

your shit slides out
yellow and
smelling of curd cheese.

At Seven a Son

In cold weather on a
garden swing, his legs
in wellingtons rising over
the winter rose trees

he sits serenely
smiling like a Thai
his coat open, his gloves
sewn to the flapping sleeves

his thin knees working
with his arms
folded about the
metal struts

as he flies up
(his hair like long
black leaves) he
lies back freely

astonished in
sunshine as serious
as a stranger he is
a bird in his own thought.

Adam

Once or twice your nightmare
woke us: your wet hair
smelling like a donkey
thin arms out you screamed
in a dream we never reached you through

But last night sober you
woke up explaining how
the curtain jerks across
another Adam face screwed up,
breaks through the glass to get you

And 'brains are funny' you say
as setting things right
we talk today. But still go on
avoiding the eye of
windows even in daylight

For a Friend under Sedation

mad girl do you still
under your skirt your small knees open brood
on the red electric bar
the tar stains there
of our tobacco shreds?

lovely at eighteen
you were always waiting
the old women
licked over
your unhappiness

last I saw you   your eyes
wider   your skin yellow   dead
black hair   your cries:
husband and two children
they said, what could you want for?

Aubade for a Scientist

To see your sadness
your lonely stupor
downstairs in a chair
asleep, your glasses
up in your hair,
your face unused

You are flying
(books at your feet and
typescript in your hand)
over the maple, the
horse chestnut: how
shall I wake you

to the tether of
these dimensions?
Symbols lie on
the paper: will you
look through their lines
and hope for crevices
open to strange light?

The Potter's Party

Where a ledge of blue
chessmen and pottery fruit
were set below a mirror

he put his hand on a
girl in wet clay and
turned her to show me

the man at her buttocks.
We were both white
with drinking and

his hair was wet: his
whisper rose to a
giggle between his teeth

     as I met in
     the stare of
     the wild glass

     black eyes of
     a face I had to
     recognise.

A Dream of Spinsterhood

'The wish for an unthinking reckless solitude' – Franz Kafka

All that Sunday
for a beginning deserts
of space
a bright self
moving single as a blade

or cruising
bodiless as a ghost
through London streets
an eye   invisible
in noise and light

But when last night
dreaming with a dry mouth
I was 25
again   alone
obsessed with sex

I cried out
caught in a
Sunday tight
as a box
and woke up weeping

to touch you in relief:
over us
leaves moved on the
ceiling gentle as
water on the roof
of a stone bridge.

New Year '66

In what premonitory
daze this New Year
races in

between these
sober houses: look,
their lightless

eyes are fixed
in a charm
as dark as

sleep is.
We are waiting for
the strangers will

release in us
a music of elation
at the next stirring

Dance for a Dead Aunt

Old aunt your
ginger hair grey
eyes are ashes

scattered: to
forget them freely
I think of you

living up North
Matron of a
hospital.   You

talked with a cigarette
smoking your nose
a spinster underneath

your clothes fastidious
lilac knickers lace
over your corset a

bosom like a bolster.
Back from Sark
you were as

clean as a
sea bird in your
lonely virtue

Now with your Will, I
read you forgive us
all   give us

(we squanderers)
what you put by
living within your pension

and how shall I
    thank you where
your lost grey sand

is shaken into
the northern air

Drunken Tuesday

Old nag I
hack on burning
with care with
hurrying stooped and
tugged at in
cold air 'money
money money'
eating at the
soft roes of the brain

Sourpuss, drag:
for what so partisan
why not put on
euphoria in a
yellow glass
so the eyes rising
like red leaves at a
windscreen give
up their witness

Run out in
rain in pools of
streetlights buzzing
with whisky, walking
at car lights
unafraid of
hoot and brake?

The black cars
wait for me when
I wake, I hear the
hiss of tyres and
the silence of
wet metal:
and the mind widens
to make out the
name of that
immunity had
seemed so gentle

Bodies

At home now   the first grey
in the hollows, morning in
the grass, in the brick
I hold you sleeping

and see last night
a bang the back door opens
holding your arm you
white say don't
be frightened smiling
your loving mouth
but white you are white

on a window a
window was it
into the flesh of your arm:
hung in the lab
in the hum of a
ship's hold, no one
to hear or help you

O you are stitched and
safe now, my fingers
feel you, I can
taste the oil in your
skin, your salty hair

knowing your blue
strings where the blood is
wanting you safe in
hard and shining steel
or tough as mineral, so
even a thin spirit of you
could be unkillable

Female Principles

For beauties delicate as twigs
see in their mirror
blades of shoulder and hip
and their eyes are eaten with desire
for sheltering flesh to
cover canal and wire
that string the throat on haggard days

And comfortable wives
feel along sides and
envy swerves of bone
pivoting cleanly
and bolt in fluttering
bulk under a silk belt

What emnity between
the fat never forgiving
twitches of other chemistry
and slender girls
shrugging off
nudges of the flesh they envy

Greenhouse

Blue stars and their
cold light of April 2 a.m.
watering these tomatoes:

Peaceful, plants are,
flowers for sex   no
moving out of their pots

green flesh   their
bruises leak a
liquid tart as smoke

and quietly our planet
fills with their
fibres

here under glass
they climb without eyes
like a rain forest

Raga

his syllables
like pebbles in a pool
their gamelan notes
       on wood and wire
their tone
       on this white leaf

A Season in Vienna

The tram grinds on
wet rails around the
corners of brown
buildings

scatheless
visitors in a
cold rain we
float your

streets of plaster
frontage pitted
down to the
brick, in

a dark afternoon
the windows burning

bemused in
electric light.

Later we had a guide
to the grandeurs
of Franz Joseph,
the *Ring*

the *Opera*, the
Kunsthistorische
and: 'On this balcony
Hitler announced

the Anschluss. Flowers
were all in bloom then
I remember:
Vienna had good springs once.'

Some Thoughts for Nathaniel

shaving in the afternoon
flesh white from sleeping
in his eyes brick streets
Midland baked brick, slate
rooves, puddles

in his ears bland
pop and bubble of
last night voices

home on a visit
he squints a red eye
hungry for what
for where
wet streets of other cities
he might stride in

for his own day
pressure

now back in his childhood
he drowns in the gaze of
his mother in a felt hat
waiting to go out shopping

and the three o'clock postman
turns his wheel
into the corner of the wind.

Idyll

The chestnut trees are massed
for rain the wind blows rain
the climbing rose is loose

and trails September leaves
as dry as finger nails
scratching across the glass

and housebound Mrs K
stares through her landing window
for her husband's Anglia

Her eyes no longer measure
the distance of a bird
and her blundering ears catch

at blood that hums in her brain
and the wind, the wind blows rain

Politics

Later the cleaners come
cigarettes pinched in their lips
as they lean gossiping

and they are gristle and bone
innocent elbows
scrubbing out urinals
with silent eyes dreaming

washing the cupboards
watching the time to be done

and the baize door is open
the torturers
are outside in the sun

Poor Relations

When my cousin married
the owner of a piece of
Leicester's Granby Street

she was perfect as the
plaster in Adderley's window.
I was about twelve

skinny and black I went
dancing at the Palais
with all the yobs on

Saturdays and lay in bed
reading on Sunday mornings:
barely polite then

all these years
after   what
has changed us?

She still lives with
a shrug, her
eyes   idle

over my long hair
and broken shoes I
recognise the

crocodile of her bag:
with some surprise we
pity one another.

Song of Power

For the baiting
children in my
son's school class who
say I am a witch:
black is the
mirror you give me

drawn inward at seige
sightless, mumbling:
criminal, to bear three
children like fruit
cannot be guarded
against enemies

Should I have lived sterile?
The word returns me.
If any supernatural power
my strangeness earns me
I now invoke, for
all Gods are

anarchic even the Jews'
outside his own laws, with
his old name
confirms me, and I
call out for the
strange ones with wild hair

all the earth over to
make their own coherence,
a fire their children
may learn to bear at last
and not burn in.

Buying a House for Now

To live here, grace
fills me like sunshine
these tall rooms

we walk through
singing: look
we have put down

a piano takes three men
to move, and
now sweeping

the pinewood floor
my mind is light
as blown glass

knowing to love what
can't be carried
is reckless

I testify
to the beauties
of now only

from Poetry Introduction 1

Marriage

Is there ever a new beginning when every
word has its ten years weight, can there be
what you call conversation between us?
Relentless you are as you push me
to dance and I lurch away from you
weeping, and yet can we bear to lie
silent under the ice together like
fish in a long winter?

A letter now from York is a reminder of
windless Rievaulx, the hillside moving through
limestone arches, in the ear's liquid the
whirr of dove notes: we were a fellowship of three
strangers walking in northern brightness, our
searches peaceful, in our silence the
resonance of stones only, any celibate
could look for such retreat, for me
it was a luxury to be insisted on
in the sight of those grass overgrown dormitories.

We have taken our shape from the
damage we do one another, gently as
bodies moving together at night, we amend
our gestures, softly we hold our places:
in the alien school morning in the
small stones of your eyes I know how
you want to be rid of us, you were
never a family man, your virtue is
lost, even alikeness deceived us
love, our spirits sprawl together
and both at last are distorted

and yet we go toward birthdays and other
marks   not wryly   not thriftily
waiting, for where shall we find it, a
joyous, a various world? in fury
we share, which keeps us, without
resignation: tender whenever we touch   what
else we share   this flesh   we
bring together   it hurts to
think of dying as we lie close

Against Winter

His kiss a bristling
beard in my ear, at 83:
'aren't you afraid of
dying?' I asked him (on his knee).
who shall excell   his shrug for answer?

and yet was it long after,
senile, he lived in our front room,
once I had to
hold a potty out for him, his
penis was pink and clean as a child

and what he remembered of
Odessa and the Europe he walked through
was gone like the language I
never learned to speak, that
gave him resistance,

and his own sense of
favour   (failed
rabbi, carpenter,
farmer in
Montreal)

and now I think
how the smell of
peppermint in his yellow
handkerchieves and the
snuffmarks under his nose

were another part of it:
his sloven grace
(stronger than abstinence) that
was the source of his
undisciplined stamina.

The Magic Apple Tree

Anniversary

Suppose I took out a slender ketch from
under the spokes of Palace pier tonight to
catch a sea going fish for you

or dressed in antique goggles and wings and
flew down through sycamore leaves into the park

or luminescent through some planetary strike
put one delicate flamingo leg over the sill of your lab

Could I surprise you? or would you insist on
keeping a pattern to link every transfiguration?

Listen, I shall have to whisper it
into your heart directly: we are all
supernatural   every day
we rise new creatures   cannot be predicted

Sundance in Sawston

In these corridors which are not my country
my gait is awkward as a scorpion:
you rise again from last night's screen, Sundance,
with a delicate snarl of insurrection
and become the dangerous dream, the
lovely fiction of   an innocent gun

spinning in sand and plaster with no blood
spilt, flippantly, you beckon us over
the long curve of tobacco earth to play
like a pair of René Clair
copains in war-time together.

Through glass through glass we look
after you up the local hill to where
in April rain the first green leaves begin.
The sun is a silver disc and this morning
is lost in a white mist.
It is English weather. Our thoughts sidle. Over
there in the whiteness   apple trees float.

In the Question of Survival

You are the white
birch tree your thought
subtle and silver as
the morning air moving in
delicate leaves

and not to traduce your
sadness: it lights
your low voice so that
sane and sequent creatures
blunder grossly in the breath
of your quiet presence

and you are a minister of grace, a
sign it is not accomplished
yet the death of the spirit: angels
move among us at first light
over the fields   mysterious
as April in the grey
wood of our garden trees.

The Magic Apple Tree

Sealed in rainlight one
November sleepwalking afternoon streets
I remembered Samuel Palmer's garden
Waterhouse in Shoreham, and at once
I knew: that the chill of wet
brown streets was no more literal
than the yellow he laid there against
his unnatural blue   because
together they worked upon me like
an icon   infantine

he called his vision   so it was
with the early makers of icons, who
worked humbly, choosing wood without resin.
They stilled their spirits before using the gold
and while the brightness held under the *kvass*
their colours too induced
the peculiar joy of abandoning restlessness

and now in streets where only white
mac or car metal catches the failing
light, if we sing of
the red and the blue and the texture of goat hair,
there is no deceit in our prophecy:
for even now our brackish waters can
be sweetened by a strange tree.

Old January

From the lattice bridge on Thursday a woman
goes in slippers over the sludge, the
snow wind parting her black hair to the skin

and as she reaches the gas-lit
passageway where music rises from
basement grids, observe: her red grin.

She is walking through an
old anger somewhere lost in
the round of her head, and when

her lips move, the words fall
like pieces of rainy sky
or stones of tourmaline.

She is a winter troll. Miriam
wild sister dance for us
our words are transparent stones

and here we are at
the northern edge of the wilderness.

Moon

At first it seems as if the
    moon governs the fen, in the waters of
many estuaries, it is felt
    even beneath the fields, in the salt mud,
and it sits in August red on
    the long flowing extensions of land into sea.

Moon, loveless and lifeless, you
    bear upon the breeding about here
uneasily; long ago crossers of
    cold seas were the very last
invasion of this region, and
    since, whole villages have fallen into
that absolute purity of race: which is incest.

And so, old clinker, still
    circling our skies, I am
your enemy: I want by some transition
    to bring in strange black
people of the sun, among
    your good and graceless villagers.
Not to do harm, only to
    have your own people remember certain
ancient songs without alarm.

I know the tyranny of landscape
    is strong, and the moon
remains entirely calm at my voice, however
    I have some disreputable allies
which even now enter the tied cottages
    by hidden electric cable.

(Yes I distrust them) Nevertheless
    true singers will complete the violation
of this area: and when they come, they
    will find your own East Anglian children
already dancing. To an alien drum.

Out

The diesel stops. It is morning. Grey sky
is falling into the mud. At the waterside
two builders' cranes are sitting like birds

and the yellow gorse pushes up
like camel-thorn between oil-drums and old cars.
Who shall I take for my holy poet

to lead me out of this plain? I want an
innocent spirit of invention: a Buster Keaton
to sail unnaturally overhead by simple leverage and

fire the machinery. Then we should all spring out of our
heads, dazzled with hope, even the white-faced ticket
collector dozing over his fag, at such an intervention

suddenly in this stopped engine, we should
see the white gulls rising out of the rain over
the fen   and know our own freedom.

100% Return Guaranteed (Advt.)

In the big black eye of the drier and
the smaller eyes which are
open circles of glass that soap and rain
a young girl is twisting under her chair

lean as a sick
mule, her skin
bloodless, her hair
long and sour that she pushes back,
she tugs at the flannel pants
of her child, roughly, transparent lips smiling

and meanwhile an invisible hand is
patiently at her white heart
squeezing and squeezing it   blue
detergent sings in the hum of the air

West

White and golden Mae
when you don't care your
childless cunning is beautiful
because you can   always move on
eyes on the next town, like a
man, cheating the system, free.

You make love of person
or place look cowed in comparison
while every turn of the seasons,
new spinach grass or even two
birds on a black tree
                    bind me

In the Matter of Miracles

(for Jimmy: nabbed again at the Elephant)

Toothless at twenty-three, fine
hair on your grey chin:
you were sitting on a
railway bench, drawn in, as
though you feared the touch of
a shoulder would scorch you

and were setting out to
London, Ireland, who
knows where
alone after a year in
the breakage and hash of
a fairy-tale revolution

at 5 a.m. that morning you were
humping our stuff out of a lorry
cheerfully, but you wondered then
and over coffee and bread afterwards
when did we think the revolution would happen?

and so as the horn sounds to vigil
this New Year we must
remember the miracles that
are daily and wholly refused,
the orbits that simply continue
perhaps for all of us?

Exile

Estonian ghosts of
river birds within the
temples of his skull, ashes
of poets, girders of school houses:
these are the tired politics
that vein his eyes

scoop a pouch under his lower
lip. In our system
his vigour has aged into
rumours of miraculous
sexual prowess, yet
the gesture of his
pasty fist is continuous with
the sag of his cardigan

and his enemies are
quiet middle-aged men, who
move in the mist of invisible
English power. He is
unhunted and unforested in the fen:
like the rest of us.

For Malcolm Lowry

Salt in the notch of my
    thumb. Lemon. *Tequila*
on my tongue. Warm and aromatic,
    juice of your cactus god.

Yet I would not filch from your
    Saint of desperate
and dangerous courses.
    Any flu-ridden and scraggy

one of us in a fever now
    can enter through your
thrown away papers into
    some Mexico of prescience.

Not *Tequila* more than gregory
    powder will I honour, but that
enormity of remaining awake, inside
    the sick pain of your head

as you went on. Choosing *words* to hold the red
    light of the heat had cracked through your
adobe skull. So they still should carry
    the last flow of your fear-sodden blood.

Onion

    Onion on the piano under the music
    yesterday I found you
    had put out fine
    green curves of new life

    hopelessly out of the earth
    the park is
    delirious with March snow
    and my mission is to remove your
    hiding place   and all places of hiding

    so that nothing can come of you
    though you consume yourself wholly:
    you are tender and green, but
        I must put you into the bin.

A Prayer for My Sons

Forgive me   bright sons   if I have hobbled
you, put my fear into you, I will
suck it out   with my   lips

spit it out   look   I will stop hiding,
see without dreaming, take the nag of
that into my spirit, live without miracles, humbly.

I want you to puzzle this planet out, this
brown planet, so you can
move with your eyes open, without lying

Please be free of me   you will
lose nothing, the dark trees will be
there at the garden's end for you still, and many songs.

Our Vegetable Love shall Grow

Shaking in white streetlight in
a cold night wind, two luminous blue fangs
push through the grass at the bus shelter:
an early crocus, drawing colour from
some hidden underfoot bulb. And now, mindless
desperate lonely waiting in a fen wind, we
barely move in our great coats, while that
blue piece of adventuring
takes all the electric of human light into
the beauty of its present flesh.

I Have Seen Worse Days Turn

However, the hot grey streets are still lit
with the flash and flicker of
overnight television, so I may
throw the morning away like
dirty water out of a cup.

Why not? Outside, the rain
and humus taste of old potatoes, which
in unfastidious hands could
blow up the whole alembic.

How do you change the weather in the blood?

Some Local Resistance

By Lammasland, this leasehold
triangle, white faces of the
lost or cumbered swim
in streets that hold the seas
of greenest librium, and
the poem may become another dream
for to let go here is to float off
blue nosed and salt water streaming

And what I mean is
to live freely in
silver light here a visitor
among birds in brown
mud splintered with ice:
to turn outward into
the cold burn of the air
to the bird with red
bars on its head under the burr

and abandon the milky
time of the lyric that lies,
to enter the somatic
world of choice: for all its danger

as at the river edge is the
white cracked wood
of that mistaken Cobbett's
imported acacia

Train Shot

going north: back through the
seasons. Cold water lies in the
grass still, grey birds rise
over trees without leaf
Here is the force of
what man has done
for the knuckled stone in
the fields and the delicate
foals he looks to   and
now turning on iron girders
over the choppy Tyne, I wonder
at these green waters
continuous with sea

Fishing

In leaf dust, and tarred wood
the chestnut, radiant as a moving tiger
the willow falling like water spilt
yellow-green in the river: my son
sits rocking eagerly, his
arms holding his knees as I
watch the bob of his float, the changes

of moving water, moving lips and his
bright eye. He is watching for
a single gudgeon to fly up
out of the silver mud, but when
he turns, smiling

in the delicate line of his
neck I sense uncertainly how
fierce a passion he
is holding back in
his still silence.

In the Dark

Who she slept with
                    was always news
and now the slur in her voice
tobacco rolled in her stubby fingers
she is dancing
motherly arms up to an old record
pointing her feet drunk
her body
            remembers the archaic gestures

Fellow-travelling

Stood there since World War I
a piece of shrapnel lodged
in his brain: under my window
he hawked and coughed in the sun
mumbling   smelly   lines of
dirt in his neck the tendons rigid
he talked to an old dog
and children on bicycles
            swerved round both of them.

Gone now: their shapes
disturb me on this street, as if
perhaps I was   a last
witness to their vanishing.

Fool Song

Free day   unmarked   open
    as though in the ochre of
river light for a breath
    even the links between the
minutes have broken

sunless in August, white
    sky, silence, skipper
butterflies: a pause

now even the most
    prudent must become as
innocent as Gimpel, mutely
    welcoming the street liar
into the room with tea, bread
    music, in quiet homage
to: discontinuity.

An Exorcism

Your gods are hostile. When you
would have them quiet
you point at me and they come buzzing
about me, you think I don't see them.

But I know them   well as you
only I don't trust them for I can tell
you how darkly they live and
how little they give to their followers

Shall we make gods of mosquitoes
that smell for our blood? Could they
ever be messengers of that other
I call holy? Many times now
I have failed to name him, and
still he offers himself

Released

In lovely rain now
this two weeks' tyranny of
sun is past and the trees

are dark   the air has
shed the dry pollens.
Now the garden follows me into

the house gently and every membrane
welcomes the soft presence.
The solar blast was a

dish of silence over me:
now I look for stars or blonde
lions in the wet undergrowth.

A New World

Two silver ghosts we cast up
to walk the deserts of silence
before us, and now their
magic is stronger than all the
scripts of the Word

They are deliberate men and
the world they govern will have
edges like moon-craters

They will neglect nothing:
and I am a
flower-murderer,
a fire-killer.

In our default
their purity will
conquer us like winter

To Cross

Nobler, they wrote on the
run   in holes   lonely
unloved
          what respite
to have an August morning green at five
young men lying in their clothes between
blankets ash about them
their unfrightened faces.
Now in this bare room
I speak with love   only
of those who keep their way in
a mad calm bearing uncertainly
the trap in which they are taken

Birthday: a Dark Morning

Waking cold   a squeeze of fear   the
muscle of the heart's entry:

and sadly sadly you cross the windy
courts stooping, my love   your shirt
floating   the rain parting your
hair to the skin   yesterday

we talked through mistakes
failures, unswept leaves in
steps to the bin   these days
wastage.   And when shall we
look again for a radiant year
or is that euphoric whiteness like
those ashen trees a
trick of the glass only,
now broken? In the
rain I pass
a milkman at the
shaft of his trailer
singing, and your
words stick in me

For this new year
no resolution will serve
unless perhaps joy   that impudence

Waiting

The house is sick. When I come down
at night to the broken kitchen, the open wall, and find
a grey-haired and courteous old
cat asleep in a design of gypsum on the ground:
I sense between iron girders and old
gas-pipes how many more ill-lit creatures of a damp
garden are waiting. Under the provisional blossom
of a plum tree they threaten a long siege
whispering: they shall eat sorrow
which is the flesh of the rat, the
dead limb in the locked room.
And I can hardly remember the dream of sunlight and
hot sweet wall-flowers that led us to break through
to the almost forgotten lord of the dark outside
whose spectres are part of his word, and whose promise of
home always demands the willingness to move on: who
forces me to acknowledge his ancient sign.

A Skeleton Puts on Flesh

Once, level with the sycamore in
    black wood of branch and bough, I could
ride out a leafless November
    like a spectral bird: not now.

Your mark is on my wrist:
    you are there in the taste of
leaf dust and rustle of
    old paper across the park.

I took your sign because
    I wanted to carry your
one muttered offer of sanctuary
    somewhere about me like a talisman

and now it brings the lemon scent
    of love into the daily and
sporadic features of default,
    defeat. And yet I understand

the timeless darkness that
    threatens, and how soon I could
feel caught again in lost hope like
    a frog in a child's hand.

Happiness

Now the grey light from the garden falls
on our bed. To be your love, sleepless
for the whisper of one night

has made me stubborn
not to die yet, not yet
though we have many faces

I carry your lips on my neck
your voice in me, this light,
morning: we can be happy, then,
without presumption

Votary

Tonight   a November fever   white
eyes of light that stare and
burn in lunatic waters. Black
city, mirror of incoherence:
here in the odours of oil cloth and the
hot soap breath of the coin laundries
is the wilderness we look for. And
though we change direction again
again these ruinous weeks, my
spirit reels with it, yet for
this moment   penniless   not caring
dazed   a piece of paper   rain-blown:
in what fierce exultation the
street sings in me.

Offering: for Marina Tsvetayeva

Through yellow fingers smoke rises about you
now we enter your transfigured life
what were those recoveries
of hope you kept to
starved ferocious ill
poet rough-clothed and cold-fingered
pushed more than loss of
lovers or even a dead child over
the edge of blackness in middle age.
When you went back to Russia   to
Efron your gentle husband   a
murderer   soon murdered   was it
in loneliness   the ear and
tongue of a language you looked for?
As misery closed in, with a last
hatred   had you
abandoned that strange trust
even when you hung yourself coldly like
an unwanted dog?   O black icon.

Lines Outward

Tell me your gods, to
what magnetic darkness
you are drawn
out of your skin
forbidden what is
it beckons or
do we look for in
the yard at 4 a.m. the
rain in the white lilac?
At these limits the
birds clattering the
steam rises from old
timbers, can we
(the planet turns)
in whose name enter it,
the lyric daze?

For The Beatles

Lived for 3 days on
coffee and bread, pinched
with the hope of getting clear
and over the radio again and
again shrewdly that electronic
track reached into me, yes
hoarsely their voices name it
the euphoric power, and the
badgered, even the mean and
the timid rise like
Japanese water flowers
in that spirit: old
impersonal rewardless *easy*
drum drum drum drum drum
Love is all you need

For Brighton, Old Bawd

Streets smelling of vinegar, fronted with junk
and monstrous sweet shops, here the sea slopes up as
bland as a green hill. And the air is a wash of

salt and brightness. This town has so transfigured
the silt of what lay in our mouths that
now we can lie happily awake together as

the first milk bottles go down on the
steps and the early lorries change gear
at the lights beneath us.

Though what is good in this city is frivolous
as the green tits on Mrs Fitzherbert's
pleasure palace, it retains the force

which is the magic of all bawdy: fit
forgiveness   that true measure   for every
shape of body and each mistaken piece of behaviour

Some Thoughts on Where

For lovely Allen   I saw you dancing
on the telly last night: a black lion.

You were lifting a monk's robe over
legs and feet at their bony male angles

smiling unforced unblown   high
over the seas that telstar moves on

you were beamed to us and we
in our local bother of where

we belong and how to   take your
airy scaling of skies as a sign

of what in the landscape of cities
has to be prized   mythic

nomad,   you live where you are   in
the now   the world you recognise is whirled in.

Grace

Not to defend
or parry, with the
closing of heart and
dead eye
          words that cross
the line of my intent

is no promise:
no one may
intend how blood
pricks most unjust
          will move who
would serve love
          to worse intransigence.

Bathroom

My legs shimmer like fish
my hair floats on the water:
tonight I observe that my
skin is no longer smooth
that blue veins show
in my arms that my
breasts are smaller

and lie seeing still water
meeting a white sky
(my elbows swim for me)
waiting for those
queer trails of thought
that move toward sleep

to where
the unforgiven words are
stored in circuits
of cells that hold
whatever shape there is
of the lost days

The Telephone, Failing Again

This public box is
the only light in the whole terrace:
a single bulb in the wet
hedge, with the wind rising.
And the harsh buzz in
my ear   carries me
over some border to where it seems
we could just
lose one another this way
like unpaired shoes in
some accident of disorder,
and I cannot even trust

you would notice the loss.
Where are you where
in what moon
house   do these dry
noises now release their dust?

Morning Car Rides

Shall I fear for you as the
farmer's children answer
the bright malice of your
logic? You are too
thin for these gestures

but your talent is not grave:
you are impudent as a
water hopper – and about
the bluntness of cruelty
need no teaching.

Daily whenever the car
pauses, meeting your eye
I puzzle at the black
disc flickering in
the blue of your eye shell

The Asthmatic

smiles and sings, in
    daylight, her
mouth curved upward
    with the taste of air.
She is sharp and joyful
    as a bird without memory

of black   gasp

and gape of broken
mouth   blood
    wheezing   for
harsh   air
    face wrung into
baby grimace, crying
    please, like a dying creature

morning   was it   the
    light strangling
behind trees or
    when did she
find herself in the hospital
    attached to a machine?

Even now she uses her night spray
and still she laughs eagerly.

A Quiet War in Leicester

the shelter,   the old washhouse
water limed the walls
we only entered once or twice
cold as a cellar we
shivered in the stare
of a bare electric light

and nothing happened:
after the war
ants got in the
sandbags
builders came

and yet at night
erotic with the
might-be of disaster
I was carried into
dreaming with delight

New Sadness/Old City

I saw Jerusalem from the Magog hills last night in
hot air the sky shaking:
white dust and crumbling stone and
the scent of scrubby hills

                                 waterless
fort   Kohelech sadly and the
Egyptian before him whispers it
the death song of triumph   the desert
powders every man's eyelashes and
his cropped hair
                             gentle city, will
the saints of the Lublin ghetto
enter your streets invisibly and
marvel at last   or fear to

as we listened like ghosts
in a parked car here breathless when
you were taken   tasting on
our teeth uneasily the strange
illicit salts of elation.

Strings

How readily now do I forgive you
Lady your hot eyes filling
behind glass your lips pursed
at my doings   like a nun
you smile towards your
husband in the hospital;
when you were ill he lay on the
floor howling and had to be doped

and 4 months later he had you typing
the office mail after the dishes
again, and dourly you sat there
spelling and phrasing for him
in that bullied quiet of yours: as
though vexed by your own endurance

Dream Flesh

Slow and easy, in a river of black water
    the curve of my shoulder rises, and
downstream in the night swim
    the shadows of trees and the
orange lights of the city

while unlit houses and their garden walls
    are falling into the weeds beneath me, as
though at night there is no barrier between
    dissolution and the daytime arrogance of
solidity. Who can believe in anything further out
    than the wet slaps at the edges of darkness?
Above me: the moving of invisible leaves.

Out of Touch

Now west down George Street a
star red as charred coal
blocks the line of the traffic

so that all the waiting cars
are made into shadows and
the street walls are red-stained

and into that March sun   you
move off lost   another shadow
against the stones of

a spectral city: love
don't be lonely   don't let us
always be leaving singly on

some bleak journey   wait for me:
this   deliberate world   is
rapidly losing its edge.

Renaissance Feb. 7

In the true weather of their art
these silver streets bustle, skin lit towers:
we have broken some magic barrier into
the daylight of the Duc de Berry's golden hours
and now in a supernatural city what is
possible changes as the
tones of tired voices lift
in the mild air
and like a tree
that might find loose birds in its
leafless hair, I am
open to the surprises of the season

The Celebrants

The Celebrants

I

Remember Melusine
morose spectre, whose own superstition once
    made a serpent of her: she was
bewitched   into a myth   by chance
    out of her housekeeping because
she was credulous, and so wandered in
    bands of the spell-bound until
she fell into encephalitic trance. And still
    to her believing company she slithered
in green skin to the last day of her life.

II

Might be anyone's cracked daughter
sozzled, or skewed of vision, lonely,
in winter months invoking mutinous powers

that pour like mercury out of the moon
into the waiting mind with its own glass-lined
pumice craters and stains of orange oxide,

always the occult temptation, the erotic
world-flicker, shining in wet streets
like coal with streaks of mica, for

the demons rise at the first oblique
longing, they rise up nocturnal and cruel, and
the neophyte becomes their stammering mouth,

breaks into joy without drugs
dangerous, cannibal, frenetic with
forbidden knowledge, in deaf violence.

Bitten with toxic spiders, women
dance themselves into exhaustion knowing
the spirits that they bear are hostile

and yet are proud to be a hostage to them,
as if their hallucinations could be
a last weapon against humiliation:

Listen to their song: as
servants of the tribe they now
enter the crisis of their terror

willing to free us from the same service,
but their song draws us after them and
some will follow   into their own unreason.

III

Trees, under wet trees, I am beckoned down to a river
that runs into land through a sink of sedge and rushes,
white trench gas, between roots galled with witches fungus
cut stumps, where bodies of bald dogs stir at the crunch of my feet.

The mud and black leaves are frozen these last hours of the
year, I follow this sloping path downwards, like a lost sleeper, in
fear of finding the faces, and hearing the voices, of those
who came this way   by the black stub alder   and under

in frost against spindle shrubs, or wych elm in tangles of
twigs, and who swim in the smoke on the stream and beneath
the rotting bridge, and float head-high in the dark evergreen
yews, and hang waiting in that poisonous foliage.

Through hoots of long-eared owl, gunshot, and cries of
mallard across the marsh, what I fear is to hear their voices;
those obdurate spirits, haunted and harrassed, who once
came down this route and laid waste their energies here

to become mares of god, crying, and singing epiphanies.
They offered their eyes and their entrails for the forest
spirits to fill them like swallow-tailed kites:
they bartered their lives and the air tastes of their drowning.

IV

In the last hour of the magus, then as now, marauding
   students went about selling horoscopes from
Lisbon to Lithuania, diseases also wandered freely
   as any demons: plague, syphilis, cholera.

The kitchens of sober doctors glittered with
   sulphur, they cast urine, read
propitious constellations and applied their
   ostrich feathers, viper fat, mummy powder.

In miniver fur, bald, with a
   sword in his pommel, tricky as any sorcerer,
Paracelsus often cured his patients,
   for which the burghers hounded him as Faustus,

because he treated the sword instead of the wound
   believing in the natural magic of
healing in the flesh, with herbs and metals
   he challenged the dominion of the stars.

For such heresy he was nearly hanged at
   Salzburg, driven out of Poland, and of
Prussia, and at the last, without any follower
   he left Switzerland

without shoes or bag or even a stick
   in token that his realm was
not of this world, and yet doubting
   what entrance he could have to any other.

V

   And this knowledge enters even
      between the bodies of lovers, though
   we share each other's vigil: that our arms

   hold water only, salt as the sea
      we come from, a spongework of
   acid chains, our innermost landscape

an arcane pulp of flexible
    chemistry; sinus, tubes,
follicles, cells that wander

from red marrow in the crevices
    of our long bones across
membranes, blood-stream, thymus,

and lymph nodes   to defend
    our separate skin-bound
unit of internal territory.

Give me your astrolabe and now tell me
    what doing or refusing kills
or how we will our bodies treachery.

VI

The red giant Antares is in Scorpio;
    in fen fields a radio dish listens.
Who will give us a horoscope for the planet?
    On December 3 which is the Day of the Emigrant,

for those who come of the ancient tribe of Habiru
    nomads, wilderness people, having no
house of their own, or magicians; my desert
    grandmother laughed at the time to come.

Since then her daughters have seen Babylon
    Persepolis, Delphi, settled in Toledo
risen, and been flung over
    the north coast of Africa as Marranos.

From Clermont, the hill of the first Crusade
    we learnt things could be good only so long.
Our poets wrote that halls in heaven opened
    only to the voice of song, but their

boldest praise was always for
    the holy stamina of body and spirit as one
which is the only sacrament will stand to
    cold, fatigue, waiting, and starvation.

VII

Lonely as a hangman through
    sweet mustard streets, at seventy
being sad and wily and austere

Buonarotti worked in fear
    for his soul, living
in prudence and squalor.

For our wood dries out,
    we shall not be
green again. In all

the bull-strong beauties of
    his torso he let in
the pressure of death,

he made it known, and
    in his dead Christ also
the full weight of strength

in a dead man. Yet where
    is the protection of
the broken body put under the ground?

VIII

Fear the millennial cities
    jasper-lit, descending
with oil and wine and corn
    from ancient prophecies,

where men with lidless eyes
    through centuries will slither
in holy crystal streets
    on the blood of massacre.

Their secret flagellant rites
    and luminous scars declare
a godhead and release
    for any follower,

but every incarnation, from
     Schmidt of Thuringia, to
the lost of our Los Angeles
     reveals itself in murder.

And only the bitch leader
     of a Jenghis pack can show
a spite   as human as   adepts
     of those who call Messiah.

IX

Today the air is cold and bitter as kale
     the sky porcelaine, the sun bleached
to white metal: I am alight with ions

awake   alert   under
     that ancient primal blue, which is
the serene accident of our atmosphere;

tethered by winter gold in
     the hair of these
bare willows on my own green waterside.

Here birds and poets may
     sing for their time
without intrusion from

either priest or physician;
     for the Lord relents; he is
faithful. In his silence.

Having no sound or name
     he cannot be conjured.
All his greatness is in this:

to free us from the
     black drama
of the magician.

Night Thoughts

Uncurtained, my long room floats on
    darkness, moored in rain,
my shelves of orange skillets
    lie out in the black grass.
Tonight I can already taste
    the wet soil of their ghosts.
And my spirit looks through the glass:
    I cannot hold on for ever.

No tenure, in garden trees, I
    hang like a leaf, and stare
at cartilaginous shapes
    my shadow their visitor.
And words cannot brazen it out.
    Nothing can hold for ever.

Green

In the resonance of that
lizard colour, mottled like stone from
Eilat, with blue fruit and patches
of mud in it: my thoughts scatter

over Europe where there is water
and sunlight in collision, and green is
the flesh of Holbein's coffined Christ, and
also the liturgical colour of heaven.

In England: green is innocent as grass.

Nachtfest

Water black water at night the Rhine and
in small boats lanterns like
coloured souls solemnly passing

into darkness, into circles of silver, into
black quick currents of water hidden as
the trees that rise over us steeply

up to the pink stone of the Munster, floating in
floodlight, Erasmus lies there lost, the leaves of
green and gold tile are shining,

fountains of white fire pour down the living
cliffs of pine, over drinking Baselers, a
mist of flies

gathers around the bulbs of the
bandstand. Now on a darkened raft held by ropes invisibly
in the centre of the river

men prepare the festival rockets, when
in spasms of red and green those sticks shoot
into the sky, their

light draws our breath upwards, we are gone
over the low moon after them into a
black imagination of depth more final than water.

The Sources

And how to praise them? Through the bad teeth of Europe we had
   tasted the breath of the Bruges canals, between old
houses, water and lichen ate into us;
   and we had slept by the waters of Köln, where
detergent fluff rises every morning from the river at sunlight.

Yet the sources are not gentle. Through the wet brown caves of
   Trümmelbach, there is a ceaseless rush of water, one solid
thrust through the mountain, listen, in that sound is the whole
   force of the planet. Yes, delicate under the
trees, quietly over stones to rock pools, shining
   between grass, sometimes in a
long slow fall of fine spray vanishing or in rain
   a smell of the soil in a night of blue lightning.
The true beauty of fall is fierce. Drenched and shaking
   what frail homage to so brutal a purity?

A Year Gone

Who believes
he is dead?
in the ground
that lies over his head
in the rain, under leaves, in the earth
who believes he is
there?

In the tick
of our blood
in the blue
muscles under our tongue
in our skulls
where a hidden ice-pick may be waiting
we must
learn

how at last
motionless
we shall fall without
breath into place

and the pain of our questions will melt like the
wax of our flesh
into silence.

A September Friend

Through your erotic landscape lit with tallow flares
grotesque and valiant lady of red eyes
you move as slowly as a boat dragged overland:
while lamed and sleepless creatures hop
after you, or fall out of your skirt.

With lonely stamina you spin the
necessary thread to hide your movements.
Why should we try to judge
your true direction? Fluently
as the grass darkens and the rain begins to
fall through sulphurous trees like strings of glass

iron wheels will roll us all underground.
Their growl is in my ears, even as I
now call up the last of your shifting images
with sadness: for you bear yourself bravely.

A Ritual Turning

(for Octavio Paz)

They shall be black metal and bone now those
treacherous and beautiful covens, tonight
I am burning a pyre of ash and
lime boughs in my heart to be rid of them,
those fingers beckoning, their
offer sweet mud in the mouth
damp, illicit. No one who
listens to that song is satisfied
until he breathes in the deathly
tars of the same intoxication.
Now I know
a man can sing with only an erotic stammer to
mark the white line of his transgression: birds
golden as weeds by the waterside return, their
delicate feet step upon green stone.
For the earth has another language, we have been
given complexities of the soil against the taste of the grave.

At the Edge

I

In your delirium your eyelids were
    raisin brown, and your beard like wet straw.
We were washed in salt on the same pillow together
    and we watched the walls change level gently as water.

But now there are white drops at the window
    this morning, in grey light, your fever gone,
do you even remember the dance of words that
    slipped between us like fish? My sober love.

II

Behind your darkness and
marooned again: I know that
island, sisters, where you wait to
offer your magenta crenellations
to some explorer, unafraid of the moon.

Yet I would bless you with no
causewayside, no mainland even,
but only more silence for you to turn in
so you receive at last whatever
light your creole petals need to open.

III

Into sleet over
stones and shells
on a visit to Winchelsea
to that lake of wet sand and sky where
the red water runs
salt from
sun into sea.

we laughed
crunching over
snow pouches to leap
at the planet's periphery
but our cries
died about us:

we were
black points upon
too inhuman a canvas
and were dwindling fast.
It was not just the Ural wind
drove us
inland for shelter.

Mas-en-Cruyes

Once
in the white powdered earth of
Provence, where the fire-winds
blow hillsides of pinebranch to ash
in your barn
where you fed us
thrush pâté and wine

we were friends:
we drank fish-soup and Pastis
alongside Cassis; in a feckless alliance
of the gross
and tenacious. I cannot remember
why we fought to be free.

But I offer
this song now, for the days lived in peace
in the twentyfour houses we've shared,
and the beauties of August,
the dry wind of Provence, and
the shelter you gave us

once   in Mas-en-Cruyes.

Survivors

In these miraculous Catalan streets, yellow
as falling barberry, and urine-scented, the
poorest Jews of Rome are at every orifice,

those that remain, the centuries have
left moneyless, and the new Romans
drive past them with a blank polaroid stare.

Even in the Synagogue their service
goes on separately in a cellar
because they came through Fez once, not directly

out of Spain. Whatever happened then
their latest dead sit in gold letters
with the rest. All that is puzzling to understand

is what the power could be that brings them out
on Friday night, after so many lessons
to laugh in garrulous Sabbath on this pavement?

'The only good life is lived without miracles.' (N. Mandelstam)

Under hot white skies, if we could,
in this city of bridges and pink stone live gratefully
here is a lacework of wooden ghosts from New Guinea
Etruscan jewels, beetles with scales of blue mineral.

Bad news follows us, however. I wonder if
anyone walks sanely in middle age. Isn't there
always some desperation for the taste of one last
miraculous fruit, that has to be pulled from the air?

Free Will

Once in a dream a graph was already
    prepared for the moment of my death:
I was present, but my flesh was
    already yellow and stiffening, I could
hardly refuse the line's black evidence.

— But who is it? I demanded: Who can lay
    a claim to so much prescience? And then
as soon as I understood the name of the enemy,
    I sprang up out of my sleep to resist.

For who knows when, or what dangerous bodily
    mechanism may be triggered by
my own concealed and cavernous treachery?

Chance

Pink and shining as a scatter of lentils
    in my sleep my broken trellis
blossomed this morning with a freak tamarisk:
    it seems my town soil has its prodigies

that cannot be willed, cannot be sown, and flourish
    in what is tired and pale but yet not seedless
as if even decay could be generous, and only
    the gardened stone fail to astonish.

Love Song

A homage to Emily Dickinson

In fluorescent white
    across a glacial sky
a weightless winter lights
    your scorched and sleepless eye

and thoughts like frozen rain, in
    brittle splinters fall
like glass into my brain,
    to spike my stubborn core.

So often at its bleakest
   your vision conquers mine,
yet quietly and quietly
   my spirits thaw again:

wet streetlights shine this
   morning, a line of minarets,
and mad quince buds on our north wall
   exact our stunned respect.

The Medium

My answer would have to be music
which is always deniable, since in my
silence, which you question, is only a landscape

of water, old trees and a few irresolute
birds. The weather is also inconstant.
Sometimes the light is golden, the leaves unseasonable.

And sometimes the ice is red, and the moon
hangs over it, peeled, like a chinese fruit.
I am sorry not to be more articulate.

When I try, the words turn ugly as rats and
disorder everything, I cannot be quiet,
I want so much to be quiet and loving

If only you wanted that. My sharpest thoughts
wait like assassins always in the dry wheat. They
chat and grin. Perhaps you should talk to them?

Lais

Lais, courtesan of Corinth, why has
Holbein given you so mild a face,
and why now does your gentle hand lie open
beside those golden coins you do not take?

Sad mother and serious, your service
must be in some way most benevolent,
a holy trimmer in this Protestant city:
you cannot hide the evidence of grace.

November Songs

I

The air is rising tonight and the leaf dust is
    burning in cadmium bars, the skinny beeches
are alight in the town fire of their own humus.
    There is oxblood in the sky. No month to be surly.

The attic cracks and clicks as we ride the night
    our bodies spiced with salt and olive sweetness:
but a savoury smoke is hanging in our hair,
    for the earth turns, and the air of the earth rises.

And it blows November spores over the sash.
    The sky is a red lichen in the mirror,
as the air rises we already breathe in the
    oracular resins of the season.

II

And now what aureole possesses the fine
    extremities of my leafless trees? They are
Florentine today, their fen wood is ochre

an afternoon's bewildering last
    sunlight honours their sunken
life with an alien radiance:

and we, who are restless by the
    same accident that gives their
vegetable patience   grace

may worship the tranquillity of
    waiting, but will not
find such blessing in the human face.

Newspaper Elegy

The cold that killed Patel
last Tuesday in the Park
by the rubbish tip
where he fell, was
nothing unnatural:

to be hungry, thin, eleven
and sit in a wet anorak
after falling in a lake
was dangerous. And our English
November air can be murderous.

Sybil

The present holder of the papers sits
behind broken glass in the derelict warehouse
androgynous, black-skulled, and ricket-boned
grimacing to deride her visitors,

skinny, tobacco-stained, alert, she has
bartered her memories of
bark smells, wild
almonds and water plants to
taste the sour air of neglected cities.

Trembling with adrenalin of
indignation, like euphoria, she
licks her lips at the modern
crystal set in the wall. Look,

it is all happening again.
We can watch together
how terror smiles through the screen
like a handsome peasant with his violin.

She sits and nods and waits for
the latest obsequies, with
a squint eye and a slant hand, she
writes: beware this generation's prophecies.

In Bed

Between rose quartz and sea-cabbage this morning
    the postman tacked towards me through
my dreams, I could hear the
    hiss of his cycle wheel approaching

but huddled deeper into my sea-bed
    to hide among the other marine creatures;
knowing envelopes below could hold
    ugly surprises in their brown manilla.

Some Unease and Angels

By the Cam

Tonight I think this landscape could
    easily swallow me: I'm smothering
in marshland, wet leaves, brown
    creepers, puddled in
rain and mud, one little gulp and

I'll be gone without a splutter
    into night, flood, November, rot and
river-scud. Scoopwheeled for drainage.
    And by winter, the fen will be brittle and
pure again, with an odd, tough, red leaf frozen
    out of its year into the ice of the gutter.

Patience

In water nothing is mean. The fugitive
enters the river, she is washed free;
her thoughts unravel like weeds of
green silk: she moves downstream
as easily as any cold-water creature

can swim between furred stones, brown
fronds, boots and tins the river holds equally.
The trees hiss overhead. She feels their shadows.
She imagines herself clean as a fish,
evasive, solitary, dumb. Her prayer:
to make peace with her own monstrous nature.

Dad

Your old hat hurts me, and those black
    fat raisins you liked to press into
my palm from your soft heavy hand:
    I see you staggering back up the path
with sacks of potatoes from some local farm,
    fresh eggs, flowers. Every day I grieve

for your great heart broken and you gone.
    You loved to watch the trees. This year
you did not see their Spring.
    The sky was freezing over the fen
as on that somewhere secretly appointed day
    you beached: cold, white-faced, shivering.

What happened, old bull, my loyal
    hoarse-voiced warrior? The hammer
blow that stopped you in your track
    and brought you to a hospital monitor
could not destroy your courage
    to the end you were
uncowed and unconcerned with pleasing anyone.

I think of you now as once again safely
    at my mother's side, the earth as
chosen as a bed, and feel most sorrow for
    all that was gentle in
my childhood buried there
    already forfeit, now forever lost.

June

Dried up old cactus
　　yellowing in several limbs
sitting on my kitchen window
　　I'd given you up for dead
but you've done it again overnight
　　with a tasselled trumpet flower
and a monstrous blare of red!
　　So it's June, June again, hot sun
birdsong and dry air;
　　we remember the desert
and the cities where grass is rare.
　　Here by the willow-green river
we lie awake in the terrace
　　because it's June, June again;
nobody wants to sleep
　　when we can rise through the beech trees
unknown and unpoliced
　　unprotected veterans
abandoning our chores
　　to sail out this month in nightgowns
as red and bold as yours;
　　because it's June, June again.
Morning will bring birdsong
　　but we've learnt on our bodies
how each Summer day is won
　　from soil, the old clay soil
and that long, cold kingdom.

Coastline

This is the landscape of the Cambrian age:
    shale, blue quartz, planes of slate streaked with
iron and lead; soapstone, spars of calcite;
    in these pools, fish are the colour of sand,
velvet crabs like weeds, prawns transparent as water.

This shore was here before man. Every tide
    the sea returns, and floats the bladderwrack.
The flower animals swell and close over creatures
    rolled-in, nerveless, sea-food, fixed and forgotten.

My two thin boys balance on Elvan Stone
    bent-backed, intent, crouched with their string and pins,
their wet feet white, lips salt, and skin wind-brown,
    watching with curiosity and compassion:
further out, Time and Chance are waiting to happen.

A City Calendar

1

In the landscape of cities
my blood moves to the seasons
in the brick and the tarmac
through old streets and alleys
moving bikes and Mercedes
flash in rain and the sun,
and miraculous trees
are the guests of my garden.

What am I doing in this chill
   city, this cold countryside,
with a bunch of fresh coriander in my basket?
   as if I didn't know these streets
will taste of mushroom and woodsmoke, fenland Autumn

always, everyone enjoys red leaves and rain, and
   nobody flinches here, not even
when, riding towards us with a bonnet hiding
   his eyes and face
oblong by oblong day the New Year approaches.

3

I can only give you   my December city
   this sodium-lit terrace and cold rain
while night flows overhead, and black trees bend
   in the flow. The birds sit heavily alone like leather sails.

If we hold together now the year is ending
   the air will soon be warn, and yellow as milk, and
even the copper husks in the garden will be green again:
   will it be in time for us, my love, in time for us?

Watersmeet

There are spores at work in the stone here, corded
   roots of dead trees holding back shale and wedged
rocks: the green foliage of the hillside conceals
   a perilous truce between plant and mineral powers

and wet-foot from the cold Lyn we climbed up
   from shining grit into fibrous barks, tall ferns
quartz in the soil, and everywhere plant flesh
   and rich ores had eaten into each other, so that

peat, rain, green leaves and August fused
    even the two of us together; we took
a new balance from the two defenceless
    kingdoms bonded in hidden warfare underfoot.

Some Unease and Angels

Even in May now with so many yellows:
    falling burberry, broom, birds with
feathers like wld tobacco, hot sun;
    some unease disturbed me, some

music of notes pitched too high even for
    dogs or prisoners, or the sick, as if there
were messengers asleep in the grass like pollen
    waiting to rise up in sudden flower

angels or darker sentinels, closing in on us
    all year, unkillable presences, they are
waiting to shrivel us even now, if we dare to
    lift their hoods and confront them without fear.

Badlands

A Letter from La Jolla

On a balcony in California
being surprised by February
which is the sweet season here, when
blue-scaled grunion dance
on their tails, at high tide
on La Jolla sands, to mate there
and are caught in pails and eaten,

I write across distance and so much time
to ask, my one-time love, what happened to you?
Since my last letter which I meant to be
cruel as my own hurt could barb it, now
under yellow skies, pale sun, I sit
sucking fresh limes and thinking over
my childish spite, and how much life I've wasted.

I'm jealous of the sensible girl
you must have married long since.
Well, I've been happy, too.
Sometimes. You always knew
the shape I'd choose would never
be single or sober, and you did not need
what you once most admired.

Unswerving as you were, I guess
you must be prosperous, your children neat,
less beautifully unruly than my own
perhaps less talented, less generous;
and you won't know my work or my new name,
nor ever read my books.
Our worlds don't meet.

And yet I doubt if you have altogether
forgotten the unsuitable dark girl
you held all weekend in your parents' flat,
talking and talking, so this letter
comes to you this morning almost in play:
our thoughts once moved so easily together
like dolphins offshore to the land mass of the day.

The Water Magician of San Diego

for Joel

A blue pool wobbles in the sun.
Above me, like ocean weeds,
the strands of palm leaves flicker;
sticky ferns unroll their fronds;
the red helicopters hum,
like summer birds overhead;
and a local voice inquires:
How are you doing today.
What can I possibly say?

I'm trying to recover, but
I haven't quite learnt the smile.
And it may take quite a while
to look out over this ocean
that covers most of the planet
and not feel mainly alone.
My neighbour in the deckchair
is a Californian male.
And he senses a foreign spirit.

My books and scribble betray it.
So far he's not alarmed.
His handsome face is dimpled.
His hair cut short as fur;
and he has no fear of failure.
Don't wish him any harm,
but I'd like to see him waver.
– Hatfield, I murmur, Hatfield.
– Don't think I follow that.

– Don't you remember him?
He doesn't, and he finds my words
both dubious and grim.
– These, I say, are the Badlands,
won back from the dry brush and buzzard
for the entrepreneur and the bandit
these old hills, (the gold hills) favour.
Nowadays the realtors
take breakfast at La Valencia.

He doesn't understand. But
my eyes are deep and burning.
My face is aquiline.
I bring a whiff of danger;
Something is out of hand.
Perhaps I've fallen into
need (or even worse) bad luck,
which are sinister contagions
nobody here laughs off.

– Shall I confess the facts?
I've lived for five years now
as love's hypochondriac, and
it's hard to break the habit.
Is that what you're picking up?
Do you guess I've carried here
some intractable history?
(I'm teasing, but his face betrays
he's sorry now he woke me.)

– Hatfield the rainmaker?
He asks uneasily.
– The same, I nod, folk hero.
A native of your city.
A farm near San Diego
housed his earliest chemistry.
I thought you'd know his name.
Once City Halls in every County
echoed to his fame.

You needed him for water
on which this coast depends.
This strip may look like Paradise
but garden life could end.
Nothing here is natural.
The ice-plant spreads magenta
but these trees aren't indigenous.
Your water's brought from Boulder
and sprinklers cool the citrus.

Which is why you need magicians
(He's looking rather pale).
You will remember Hamelin?
No. Europe is far away.
The burghers learnt a lesson there.
Magicians must be paid.
Comfort and complacency
bring in their own revenge
– The whole thing's superstition!

– No doubt, I nod to this,
And yet his contracts were fulfilled.
The clouds formed as he promised,
the reservoirs were filled.
He was modest in his offer
to those areas parched for rain;
set evaporating tanks about,
his only claim, within a month,
Nature would end the drought.

He came when men were waiting.
Made an educated bet.
The councillors who hired him
must have known as much, and yet
they paid their fifty dollars out
with unconcealed relief.
The snag in San Diego
was the absence of belief.

Newspapers counted down the days
and gloated as they passed.
For being taken in, they mocked
the Mayor and all his staff.
(The charlatan's forgiven here
but no one trusts a victim.)
Lawyers sent to Hatfield
made manoeuvres which he met

with sardonic understanding,
and at once planned his departure.
The careful and the sober
should treat with great respect
whoever lives upon his wits.
Con-men, poker-players, poets
put the solid world at risk
and then enjoy the dance;
what happened then was in excess
of meteorological variance.

Rain? More than sixteen inches.
Flooded freeways, and carried off bridges.
There were bungalows dragged off their moorings.
And houses perched up on the cliff edge.
There was furniture floating on drainage.
There were hailstones like hens' eggs, and flashes
that carved out a creek through the desert.
Then mass panic.
Evacuation.

Abandoning motorised transport,
in rowboats, on surf boards and planks
the rich mostly got away early
but they couldn't call in at the banks.
My neighbour said with conviction:
– They'd have lynched him!
But I shook my head: It seems
Hatfield's contracts continued.
And the law wasn't ever called in.

My neighbour can't lie in his deckchair.
Perhaps he should take a quick swim?
Or calm his nerves in the Jacuzzi.
I feel almost friendly to him.
– Three wives, I should guess, lie behind you.
You're rich and you're healthy, and free.
Don't be anxious
or look for an answer
to some threat you imagine in me.

If I ever succeed in escaping
from this future where I am a stranger
and find myself back home in Europe
with those I most love out of danger;
as I fly back on some scheduled airline
(putting all my old pennies together)
when my spirit revives, I may well be
peppery, bold and alert there.
But I won't interfere with the weather.

Home

Where is that I wonder?
Is it the book-packed house we plan to sell
with the pale green room above the river,
the shelves of icons, agate, Eilat stone
the Kathe Kollwitz and the Samuel Palmer?

Or my huge childhood house
oak-floored, the rugs of Autumn colours, slabs of coal
in an open hearth, high-windowed rooms,
outside, the sunken garden, lavender, herbs
and trees of Victoria plum.

Last night I dreamed of
my dead father, white-faced, papery-skinned
and frailer than he died. I asked him:
– Doesn't all this belong to us? He shook his head,
bewildered. I was disappointed,

but though I woke with salt on my lips then
and a hoarse throat, somewhere between
the ocean and the desert, in an immense
Mexico of the spirit, I remembered
with joy and love my other ties of blood.

Remembering Brecht

'The man who laughs has not yet heard the appalling news'

That April, even though the trees were grey
           with something more than winter, when
I heard your voice and felt the first tremor
           of recovery, my joy was most mistaken,

which is not to say that living clenched with terror
           offers any protection. Other surprises
wait upon tears. Whatever we devise
           things may get worse.

Don't cry.   They often do.

Regret

Do not look backward, children.
A sticky burning sea still lies below.
The harsh air stings like sand

and here among these salty pillars
the unforgiving stand. Take
the mountain ledge, even though

it crumbles into dust. Walk or crawl,
you must let the rocks cut into your feet without pity.
And forget the smoking city. God punishes regret.

England

Forgotten, shabby and long time abandoned
    in stubbled fur, with broken
teeth like toggles, the old gods are leaving.
    They will no longer crack the
tarmac of the language, open generous
    rivers, heal our scoured thoughts.
They will only blink, and move on, and
    tomorrow no one will remember their songs

unless they rise in warning, as when
    sudden planes speed overhead
crossing the sky with harsh accelerating
    screams. You may shiver then
to hear the music of the gods leaving.
    This generation
is waiting for the boy Octavius.
    They don't like losers.
And the gods are leaving us.

Rose

Your pantry stocked with sweet cooked fish,
    pink herring, Polish cucumbers
in newspaper, and on the gas
    a bristly hen still boiling into soup:
most gentle sloven, how I honour now
    all your enormous, unfastidious welcome.

And when the string of two brown carrier bags
    bit into your short fat fingers
you only muttered, doesn't matter
    doesn't matter. I didn't understand
why you continued living with a man
    who could not forgive you, could not

forgive your worst offence:
   your happiness in little.
Even a string of shells would give you pleasure,
   but we did not bring gifts often;
and now it is too late to thank you for
   the warmth of your wide bosom, and the dimpled arms
waiting to hug my own bewildered children.

The Old Tailor

      Yellow and bitter even
when we first met I remember:
   lenses, already thick and insectivorous,
turning upon me their
      suspicious glare.

      Your legend was familiar to me:
the sourlipped snarls your
plucky wife smiled through,
   the harshest sneers for
anyone rash enough to take you on.

I wonder, now, how miserable you were,
   a clever child at school,
forced out to work. When did you first put on
   that brutal mask of blind
ferocity, to hide the lonely certainty of failure?

Remembering Jean Rhys

– Is that the new moon, that
    fine white line on the night, look,
through the hotel window? Then she covered up
    enormous eyes, to hide the dangerous sign.
And some cowardice made me lie.

Too much ill-luck had already happened,
    I suppose. Now, in her seventies, however late,
I wanted her to be having a fling and a treat
    unworried by some message from the skies
she might believe.

She listened for a moment like a child,
    smiling, and yet I saw
under the blue credulity of her gaze
    a writer's spirit,
and that was not deceived.

Wild Fruit

Yesterday, I found an over-ripe quince,
    wrinkled and yellow, on the tree
and the sweet flesh smelled of
    stored apples in a half-remembered room

from a childhood as far off as another country,
    where the light was golden as
weeds by an autumn waterside, and all
    that pungent garden entered the house

and breathed its warmth in fruit. And I
    held to the memory all afternoon, even though
the whole fen sky glared white,
    and the thin November air tasted of snow.

Park Parade, Cambridge

in memory of Elizabeth Bishop

Your thoughts in later years must, sometimes,
have visited this one-time lodging house,
the wood then chocolate brown, the plaster
veined, this bedroom floating over
spongy grass down to a shallow river.

As a mild ghost, then, look with me tonight
under this slant roof out to where
the great oak lies, its foliage disguised
with flakes of light. Above us, clouds
in these wide skies remain as still as sandbars.

Sleeplessly, together, we can listen
to the quiet song of water, hidden
at the lock, and wait up for the first
hiss of cycle tyres and whistling builders.
Fellow asthmatics, we won't even cough

because for once my lungs are clean,
and you no longer need to fight for breath.
And though it is by chance now I inherit
this room, I shall draw both tenderness and strength
from the friendly toughness of your spirit.

Hamburg

for Martin

You gave us all the riches of the city;
opera, pool-halls, all-night
Café Stern, cold Pils, and laughter;
the taste of coffee
with the first newspapers

and Isestrasse, over the canal,
street market stalls piled up
with edible truffles, beans
of black locust, poppy-seed buns,
and living fish.

We watched three carp swim there
in a glass tank; and knew
the bite of each grim
Asian jaw was meant to crush no more
than muddy weeds against a horny palate,

fierce yet vegetarian.
When the strongest fish leapt out
slap at our feet, it was your hand
that checked my squeamish terror.
My bold son,

learning to live without protection now
other than grace and beauty,
how I bless your spirit, as I
call up voice and face
to give me courage in this lonely place.

New Year

Blue velvet, white satin, bone horn: once again
We are summoned today to consider mistakes and failures
into the shabby synagogue on Thompson's Lane.
Shopkeepers, scholars, children and middle-aged strangers
are gathering to mumble the ancient prayers,

because this is Rosh Hashonah, the New Year,
we have all come in out of the Cambridge streets
to look around and recognise the faces
of friends we almost think of as relations
and lost relations who never lived anywhere near.

How are we Jewish, and what brings us together
in this most puritan of protestant centres?
Are the others talking to God, or do they remember
filial duties, or are they puzzled
themselves at the nature of being displaced?

I sit and think of the love between brothers,
my sons, who never took to festivals
happily seated round a family table;
I remember their laughter rising up to my bedroom,
late at night, playing music and cards together.

And as I look back on too many surprises
and face up to next year's uncertainties,
somehow I find it easier and easier
to pray. And this September, hope at least for
perfumes rising from a scrubby hedge
if not from flowering Birds of Paradise.

New Songs for Dido and Aeneas

1

The day opens, bland
and milky-blue. A woman
is looking out at a rain-washed garden.
In her thought a wooden flute and
spice trees, and the sun
flashing off the bracelet at her wrist.
She is no longer waiting for something to happen.

Her quiet face observes
the evidence of an order
older than Greece, in whose protection
the courtyard holds the trees, and
all her memories stir as gently
as leaves that flicker on the wall below her:

A stranger already knocks at the gate of the palace.

2

After Europe, Dido, all winter
the days rushed through me
as if I were dead, the
brown sea pouring into the cities
at night, the rain-smell of fish,

and when you ask for my story, how
we came to be blown along your
dock-streets, pocked and scuffed,
I see only my mother laced in silk,
myopic, her small feet picking over rubble.

How to make you imagine
our squares and streets, the glass
like falls of water, the gold-leaf
in the opera houses. There were
summer birds golden as weeds,

the scent of coffee and halva
rising from marble tables,
and on dark afternoons
the trams grinding on wet rails
round the corners of plaster palaces

such a babble of Empire
now extinguished, we can
never go home, Dido,
only ghosts remain
to know that we exist.

3

Some pain has burnt a desert in your head,
   which spills into the room,
sexless and stony-eyed, you rock
   over the landscape of your sandy dead.

I cannot soothe or reach into your dream
   or recognise the ghosts you name, or even
nurse your shaken body into calm.
   You wake, exhausted: to meet daylight in hell,

as the damned wake up with pennies
   of departure, and the ash
of all their lives have left undone
   lying like talcum on the tongue.

4

Unrepentant, treacherous, lecherous
   we loved beauty, in the tenderness
of violins, or the gentle voice of a girl,
     but we built over the stink of our dead,
our rivers ran yellow with the forgotten.
     Dido, the cruel cannot be blessed.

This endless sunshine, frangipani, gulls calling:
     How can you ease my pain or give me rest?
Ours was the generation that opened the gates
     to all the filthy creatures that had waited
for centuries to lay our cities waste.
     Your village kingdom cannot heal me now.
In any case, the cruel cannot be blessed.

Things come too late to save.
     On the last boat, we sang
old prayers, and some dreamed of quiet,
     but the sea took most of us. And
I am not prepared for white soot, cold ash,
     or the red sands of Australia. Forget me,
Dido. The cruel cannot be blessed.

5

     Back from the seashore
        plangent, uncertain;
     speaking of duties,
        but weaker, frightened.

     The monster you found
        so gentle a beauty, is
     no stranger here to us.
        You call her Venus;

but she is a mollusc
   goddess, pink in orifice,
prey clamped sweetly
   deep inside her ocean flesh.

What good mother would
   throw you to the ruthless seas?
Only the harshest
   and meanest of the deities.

You speak of yellow afternoons,
   dark skies, wet streets. And I who
once let the whole building of my own
   kingdom stop, to care for you,

offer my counsel; since
   it is in my gift
to curse or bless: be prudent, for
   you put us both in peril.

6

Last night, my sad Creusa, quietly
   crept into my dream. As if
dry leaves could speak, she whispered,
   but I could not catch her words,
Dido, and I was afraid

of what had wakened her.
   She was a loyal wife, in times
when nothing was forbidden
   no pleasure thought too gross:
and contrition as poor-spirited as cowardice.

Shall I spread that disease
   over the known world in a single colour?
Dido, I swear that Venus' weather in the cave
   the day our mouths first opened to each other,
and sweetness ran m our veins, was innocent.

Monsters and blood I dream of now.
and a long voyage, lost,
although the wind has filled our sails.
I must not falter in my mission,
Dido, at whatever cost.

7

Now in your leaving I admit old age.
How else? a clutch of whiteness at the heart
dry lips and icy wrists, a scream
that cuts my face into a wooden gape

At night   awake   alone   alert
to cries of meat-eating birds,
the whinge of gristle on bone, I sit
propped up on pillows, choking

on the catarrh of tears.
Sick   and yet stubborn
I, who was once your nurse,
hold back the power of my ancient curse.

8

Now we leave harbour, I no longer
fear the years' exile
nor what serenity I've lost:
I shall be no footnote now or gloss.
Empire is mine.

New heirs will rise to impose their will
on strange planets that all still
remain unknown, and thus fulfil
my deepest lust.

In this I trust.

9

The pyre of pine
and flex is prepared
and moonlit herbs
isn't that the tale
of Dido's final stroke
to wet Aeneas' eyes
as smoke?

European lies:
I come of harsher blood
long ago, the venom of
scorpions ceased to harm
and I've learnt from
cactus and desert grass
what to do without.

I recognise in you that
juniper tree, top-heavy
with branches, who may be
will try to seed
again in parched earth
and salt land;
but will not stand.

While my own root
goes deep, into soil where
mysterious waters keep their
sources cool, and though my leaves
dry out, and the wild sands blow,
I shall live my time.

And when my bones lie
between white stones at last
and fine white dust
rises over all, no one who
survives among the dead
will scorn my ghost.

Three Songs from Ithaca

1

My man is lost.
And yet his wisdom sings in my
innermost source of blood,
my flesh recalls his love.
We were one earth.

I hold the pain,
as I wait every day
to question sailors at the port,
and so endure their sly reports
of his delay.

No more than water
once to his moods,
even now though he lies
on a foreign coast,
I am drawn and pure;

and on his return
I shall bless the sea
and forgive whoever holds him
far away from me.
If he only lives.

2

Yet I sit stubborn here
as the granite of his kingdom.
My house is at risk
and my son within,
and I shall not abandon it.

Ithaca, his home, where else
should he look to find me?
Every night as I am weaving and waiting,
I call up the powers of
a helpless woman

praying for happiness,
Odysseus, as you rush on, unlit,
into the inner and
the under darkness where
all our dreams meet.

3

Who brings a message over
the threshold of my dream? It is
Hermes, the twister, the pivoter, to remind me
of strangers, returning, who speak in the language
of timberwolves, feeding on human flesh, sorcerer's prey.
And I blench at his voice.

But I straighten awake.
Even if he is sick, huddled up,
with a grey face and seamed, my old love,
looking fierce or mad, my
Odysseus, bitter or black, I am his,
as I held back my own death for this:
so now I rejoice.

Songs of Eurydice

1

The dead are strong.
That winter as you wandered,
    the cold continued, still
the brightness cut
    my shape into the snow:
I would have let you go.

    Your mother blew
my dust into your lips
    a powder white as cocaine,
my name, runs to your nerves
    and now I move again in your song.
You will not let me go.

The dead are strong.
Although in darkness I was lost
    and had forgotten all pain
long ago: in your song
    my lit face remains
and so we go

    over pools that crack
like glass, through forests shining
    black with twigs that wait
for you to wake them, I return
    in your praise, as Eurydice's
ghost I light the trees.

    The dead are strong.

2

River, green river, forget
    your worm-eaten gods,
for we come to sweeten you,
    feel how the air has grown
warm and wet now
    the winds have all fallen.

On bent willow boughs
    beads of yellow break open
winter creatures we roused
    giant beeches and scrubland
in white roots respond
    Orpheus   Orpheus

We release all the woodlands
    from sleep, and the predator birds
from their hungering,
    wild cats are calm
as we pass

as we reach the fields
men with grey knuckles
    lean over furrows
and blink.
    In the villages

wives honed too thin
    with their riverside washing
now straighten up,
    listen and nod.
What are they remembering?

    In cities, the traders
leave market stalls; even
    the rich leave their
food tureens. No one
    collects or cleans
their dirty crockery.

    Click! All transistors off.
Traffic stops. In
    a voice, everyone
hears how much
    any soul touched
by such magic is human

3

A path of cinders, I remember
    and limping upward
not yet uprooted from
    my dream, a ghost

with matted eyes, air-sacs
    rasping, white
brain, I staggered
    after you

Orpheus, when you first
    called, I pushed
the sweet earth from my mouth
    and sucked in

all the powders of volcanic ash
    to follow you
obedient up
    the crumbling slope

to the very last ridge –
    where I saw clumps of
yellow camomile in the dunes
    and heard the applause

of your wild mother
    great Calliope
crying good, my son, good
    in the fumes of the crater.

When the wiring sputtered
    at my wedding feast
she was hectic, glittering;
    her Arabian glass

burst into darkness
    and her flesh shimmered.
She was still laughing, there,
    on that pumice edge

with all Apollo's day behind her
    as I saw your heavy
shoulders turn. Your lips move.
    Then your eyes.

and I lay choking   Orpheus
    what hurt most then was
your stunned face
    lost

cruel   never to be touched
    again,   and watching
a blown leaf in your
    murderous eye

shrivel ...

4

A storyteller cannot depict
even a tree without
   wind and weather: in your song

I was changed and reborn.
   When you asked for my innermost
thoughts, once, they lapped

   under shadows in shallows,
I never could find them:
   you wanted my soul,

water creature I was, all my life
   I had loved you in silence:
it was not what you wanted.

   My thoughts flew through pebbles
alight with the flash
   of my silvery sisters

in whispers between us.
   You wanted my soul,
though I shivered and bleached,

   and it slipped from us both
when the snake bit my foot
   I was white as a moth.

In your song I am whole.

5

Over many centuries
modest ladies
who long for splendour
        gather here

their eyes most tender
their voices low
and their skins still clear
        when they appear

and to Dionysus
they offer their bodies
          for what they seek

The god of abandon
destroys their reason
          Beware the meek!

                    6

You belonged to Apollo
     the gold one the cold one
and you were his servant:
     he could not protect you.

You called for your mother
     and her holy sisters
she wept as a witness:
     but could not protect you.

Here they come, murderers,
     their bodies spattered
with blood as they stagger
     off-balance towards you.

They claw and maul you
     with hoes and long mattocks
their heavy rakes tear at your
     throat and your fingers.

They batter the listening
     birds, and the oxen
at plough, and they share out
     the limbs of each creature they kill.

Any my love's head is thrown
     on the waters, it floats
singing still. All the
     nine Muses mourn,

Orpheus   Orpheus –
     for how many poets
must die at the hands
     of such revellers?

7

And the curse of all future
    poets to die by
rope or stake or fire falls there
    on these mindless creatures

no longer human their toes
    grow roots and their knees are
gnarled – their arms branch leaves:
    who will release them?

Their flesh is wood.

8

    As dreamers now together
we forget Apollo's day
    that cruel light in which at last
all men become shadows;
    and we forgive even those
dead gods, who sleep among us.
    For all their gifts, not one
of them has power to summon us.
    In this green silence
we conceal our one true marriage.

City Music

Urban Lyric

The gaunt lady of the service wash
stands on the threshold and blinks in the sunlight.

Her face is yellow in its frizz of hair
and yet she smiles as if she were fortunate.

She listens to the hum of cars passing
as if she were on a country lane in summer,

or as if the tall trees edging this
busy street scattered blessings on her.

Last month they cut a cancer out of her throat.
This morning she tastes sunshine in the dusty air.

And she is made alert to the day's beauty,
as if her terror had wakened poetry.

Annus Mirabilis 1989

Ten years ago, beneath the Hotel Astoria,
    we watched a dissident cabaret in Budapest,
where they showed Einstein as a Jewish tailor.
    All the women on stage were elegantly dressed.

Their silken garments were cleverly slit to expose
    illicit glimpses of delicate thighs and breast.
Einstein was covered with chalk, in ill-fitting clothes;
    he was taking measurements, trying to please the rest.

At the climax of the play, to applause and laughter
    they raked him with strobe lights and the noise of guns.
I was chilled by the audience euphoria.
    Of course, I don't have a word of Hungarian,

and afterwards there were embarrassed explanations,
   which left out tailoring and obsequious gestures.
Their indignation was all about nuclear science, while
   I pondered the resilience of an old monster.

Infidelities

Last night she ran out barefoot over
the wet gravel to call him back
from the street. This morning,
in the tranquillity of bath water,

she wonders when it was she first shivered
with the wish for more than ordinary happiness.
How did she fall in love with poetry
that clear eyed girl she was?

Late at night, by a one-bar heater,
her unpainted lips parted
on the words of dead poets.
She was safer in the dance hall.

'And if you can't love poetry,'
she muses. 'What was there of me
all those years ago, apart from
that life of which it is made?

Only an inhospitable hostess,
a young woman in an old dress.'

A Favourite Uncle

In your Bing Crosby blazer, you were
handsome and clean, and smelled of lavender.

When I kept trying to kirby grip
my electric brown hair away from my face,

you showed me how to comb it loose.
My aunts dived like seals into the cold sea

on Southport sands. Your gentle grip checked me
in salty wind to have me listen to

a scratch string band, and steered
my bony elbow with a courteous gesture.

At ninety now you use that same pressure
crossing your Bootle street, and I feel again

like a child that could rely on male protection.
I can't, because I have not lived as I should,

and you need my help these days, being confused
by a town, you say, is always being moved

around your tall Victorian house that stands
anomalous among the shopping malls.

Convalescence

These yellow afternoons, dark skies, wet streets.
Only the harshest taste reaches through to me.
Nothing I read bites in. My Jules Verne
window seat noses a sunken world
of willows dragging in muggy air and
flowers drowning in mud, skidding
a bridged river, skips of rubble,
dead osiers. The days run under me.
Tock.   Tock.
I count them. Even as I feel
beneath my nightgown quietly
flesh pinched together like dough
begin to crust and heal.

Going Back to Cambridge

There they all are on the lawn
in warm air sweet as milk
eating strawberries on the grass.

I remember them awkward and young:
the men with scuffed leather elbows,
the women carelessly dressed.

The men are in dark suits now;
they have Chairs, they are part of
The Royal Society's Fellowship,

one has been knighted, yet I wonder if
any of our adolescent selves
would have been delighted

to see how far we have moved from that shabby
city of leaky gas fires and broken lino
which so bewitched our spirits long ago.

Childhood Tyranny

It must have been 3 am when she said to me
'No point in going to sleep.

As soon as we drop off, that alarm
will ring and it'll be time for school.'

I was so tired, I couldn't even reply
but my body wouldn't be pinched awake:

for my forensic skill poor evidence.
The body wisely has its own defence.

Photographs

At twelve I didn't like my own face, because
my eyes were huge and open as a dog's,
and I wanted slitty eyes like Virginia Mayo.

Photographs show me laughing and healthy,
with wide shoulders and strong wrists that could take me
up the pear tree to the highest boughs.

Between these brown card covers adolescence
stirs. 'Oh Daddy,' I asked once
'why aren't I prettier?' He was kindly but embarrassed.

Now I look back on photographs of that girl
as if I were already some ginger haired ghost
visiting a sepia world of strangers,

and among so many faces I like most
her laughter lines, strong nose and windblown hair.
And if I could fly back I should whisper to her

where she stands, painted and scared in the dance hall
setting out her sexual wares: What you
think of as disadvantages will bring you through.

Hay Fever

When Timothy grass and Rye pollen flew
each year, I began to honk like a goose.

It was always summer and party time
for kissing and rolling in the grass

so I couldn't bear to stay at home in bed.
I painted my face with beige pancake

put drops in my eyes, and learnt instead
as my membranes flared and I gasped for air

how to feel out of things
even when there.

Valentine for a Middle-aged Spouse

Dear Love, since we might both be dead by now
through war, disease, hijack or accident
at least for one day let's not speak of how
much we have bickered, botched and badly spent.
Wouldn't it make much more sense to collude
in an affectionate work of camouflage,
turning our eyes away from all we've skewed
to the small gains of household bricolage?
As our teeth loosen and our faces crag
(I shall grow skinnier as you grow paunched,
a Laurel to your Hardy, not much brag),
I'll think of all our love most sweetly launched
if you will look with favour on these lines
we may still live as tender valentines.

Homecoming

The light is sullen today, yet people are
bustling in the rainy street under my window,

poking in the Cypriot grocers for aubergines,
buying their strings of garlic and onions;

they can choose between the many seeds on
the bread: rye, sesame, cumin.

Across the road, the pharmacy windows
are lettered in brass like a Victorian shop.

In the coffee house with its heavy green and gold
pottery, they serve bean soup with sausages

and the accents of old Vienna mingle
with California. In the countryside

every one of us would be found peculiar.
We'd leak away. In Englands Lane

(through road for taxis and the Camden hoppa)
this city music and a few friends keep me sane.

Snowy Landscapes

Yesterday, I flew in over the landscape
my grandfather tried to farm near Montreal.
There was ice in the stubble, hard snow
and flat spaces that made me flinch
to imagine the winter below.

Now in mountain country in Colorado
the snow's whiteness has us catching our breath,
rejoicing at the violence of sunlight here;
and even at night when so many storms gather
enjoying the flash on the snow.

Why do mountains soothe us? They should alarm.
Instead, their snows seem to induce in us
a queer spirit of compassionate calm:
as if their beauty lit our thought so sharply
we become equal to the threat of harm.

Getting Older

The first surprise: I like it.
Whatever happens now, some things
that used to terrify have not:

I didn't die young, for instance. Or lose
my only love. My three children
never had to run away from anyone.

Don't tell me this gratitude is complacent.
We all approach the edge of the same blackness
which for me is silent.

Knowing as much sharpens
my delight in January freesia,
hot coffee, winter sunlight. So we say

as we lie close on some gentle occasion:
every day won from such
darkness is a celebration.

Aviation

Tonight our bodies lie unused like clothes flung
    over a bed. I can taste brown rain.
Flat land, wet land, I can feel your winter
    seeping into my blood like an old sickness.
This is your season of waiting and warm convalescence
    when restful spirits can be quiet and gentle
Why am I feverish then, what are these
    troubled insomniac beckonings?
What are they to me, the islands where
    falcons breed, or green rivers
where red mullet and shad swim up from the sea?

I have a monster in my head, yellow
    and surly as a camel, an old woman
clutching a hot bottle against the damp,
    and I recognise her face. She frightens me,
more than the loneliness of being awake in the dark.
    And so I put on skinny leather wings and my
home-made cage of basket wear and start
    my crazy flapping run. In this light
I must look like an old enthusiast in
    daguerreotype. These marshlands
clog the feet. I know, and then
    I may not rise, but all night long I run.

Debts to Marina Tsvetayeva

Tough as canvas, Marina, your soul
was stretched out once against the gale
and now your words have become sails.
You travel far into a darkness
I don't plead for since I can't aspire
to join your spirit on that Christian
star whose fire is green and cool
in your imagination of heaven.

Mothers, Marina, yours and mine, would
have recognised a bleak and dutiful spirit
in each other: we were supposed to
conquer the worlds they had renounced.
Instead, we served poetry, neither of us
prepared either for marriage or the solitary life.
Yours was the lyric voice of abandon
only sobered by poverty and homesickness.
Once or twice I felt the same loneliness,

but I can never learn from you, Marina,
since poetry is always a question of language,
though I have often turned to you in thought as if
your certainties could teach me how to bear
the littleness of what we are on our own
without books, or music, or even a pen;
or as if your stern assurance of the spirit
could preserve us on that ocean we sail alone.

Blasphemy Laws

Today the plump flesh of a white crocus
has broken through the dry earth at the tube station,

and the dusty hedges on Haverstock Hill
have begun to put out pale new leaf.

Their ungardened roots are responding
to the inner code and motion of the planet

both forces clearly independent of us.
Doesn't a law to protect God seem blasphemous?

Blue Snow

It was a winter evening
on quiet streets, a young girl
running in broken shoes

over the snow. She goes
hurrying to a lover,
to heal their quarrel.

Her hot face is wet
with a fever of 102°.
Next week, in the hospital,

she whispers again and again:
'your lips are salt' and
'the snow is blue.'

Circe's Island

Circe, he called me, as if
he had thrown away the onward
movement of his life

to lie within my arms, as if
my inner dream had
damaged him.

Is it possible? I thought to be
Penelope weaving stories
to furnish a cold house.

I argue, Circe was wronged.
She did not poison but enchant
spirits of those who lost their way.

I claim no drug persuaded
Odysseus to take his ease
so long beneath her sweet spice trees.

But I know myths are dangerous.
All the harm is done,
and these ten years are gone.

And how can I console him,
my broken-hearted prince,
for his lost kingdom?

Muse

for E. T.

'Write something every day,' she said,
'even if it's only a line,
it will protect you.'

How should this be?
Poetry opens no cell,
heals no hurt body,

brings back no lover,
altogether, poetry is
powerless as grass.

How then should it defend us?
Only by strengthening
our fierce and obstinate centres.

Dignity

An old poet has come to the Festival,
his books lie over the table, we all

marvel at him. He is already sure
of his place in the history of literature.

I watch his weariness, the way
his eyes flicker without envy

over the students with everything still to do.
Against probabilities, I should like to

believe in the perfection of his life
yet I observe: he has a young wife.

Songs from Plays

Songs from The Bet

An opera for puppets

The Puppet Opera, 'The Bet', was first performed
at the Purcell Room in July 1990, and went on
to the Almeida Theatre in the same month.

Argument

When the son of an old widow leaves home to seek
his fortune, she gives him a ring and makes him
promise not to part with it. After he's gone,
a wandering Spirit of Unhappiness visits the widow.
The Spirit makes a bet with the widow that her son can
be persuaded to part with the ring. If the widow
wins she may have anything she desires. If she
loses she must give up her hope. The Spirit adopts
several disguises and tries to tempt the boy to part
with the ring, first through fear, then through greed,
and at last through love.

The Widow's Song

I used to enjoy being quiet and alone,
Making jam, or choosing colours for my weaving,
Potting hares, or baking roots, I always hummed a song,
And I never had the time for grieving.
But now there's no one needing my attention,
It's as much as I can do to keep
The larder clean, and sweep ...

Look at the soup that's on the table.
The pan it comes from stands completely empty.
There isn't one last drop left on the ladle.
I promise you there's nothing in the pantry.
There's nothing in this hut.
No food left and no wood.
How can I make a bet?
I've no food for the morning,
And no goods to sell.
How can I make a bet?

The Ring

Here is a ring that isn't worth much money.
I've never been entirely sure it's silver
The stone is malachite, which may be lucky
So take it now and put it on your finger.
Remember just one thing –
Don't give away the ring!

Think of it as a sign of my affection
Your father, whom I loved, gave it to me.
I always thought of his love as protection
While you are gone, I'll pray for your safe journey
Just promise me one thing,
Don't give away the ring.

Song of the Spirit of Unhappiness

Look at how delicate and frail I am!
In my large eyes are pools of need.
How much I need, how little I expect to have.
I draw the life from everyone I meet.

Look at the darkness in my dangerous eyes,
And see the longing of my empty soul.
I'm looking for a treasure I will recognise,
When it makes my poor unhappy spirit whole.

What the Spirit of Unhappiness Wants

Hope cheers the farmer when the sky is red.
Hope saves the lost man when the moors are misty.
Hope gets the poor man out of bed
And keeps him going when the days are grisly.

And what you have is Hope in real abundance.
You wake with Hope each morning, like a miracle.
Whatever else, your hand has never lost that thread
What you have that I don't is Hope ... it's simple!

Song of the Forest

He's made a fire to warm him
And dreams of childhood play,
Of snowballs and toboggans,
Hot pies and happy days.

Nothing now disturbs his rest.
No fear of the dark place.
Cold moonlight in the forest,
Hardly reaches his young face.

Painted City Song

The shop windows of the city glitter daily
With pairs of satin shoes on heels like spiders,
Gold capes, and veils of silver lace, and jewels.
Rich people in their furs survey them grandly.
And for what it cost to buy a pair of curtains,
You could live for two good years in the mountains.

From The Temptation of William Fosters

In Praise of Gift Horses

Some people treat my best gifts with suspicion
Some fears are learnt as early as the font.
You think the Devil's just a superstition
yet still go on refusing what you want.

Let's say ...
Some fellow finds himself
back in the slammer
and some nark suggests
a way he can be free:
he'd be well advised to take
the chance and stammer:
'Yes, I'd like to be outside
in the sunshine with my bride,'
and not look sourly at the offered key.

Let's say ...
You find some massive
banking error
leaves your overdraft
some thousands to the good.
No one is hurt by that,
so where's the terror?
Surely any family man
will take a fortune when he can?
Don't hesitate, I say. Nobody should.

It's true that long ago ...
there was some hanky-panky
in a shower of heavenly gold.
And if the Trojans hadn't pulled
that horse in, Ulysses'
plan would have been foiled.
But you must see all that makes
those acts immoral are – mistakes!
Fear the disaster, not the offer, frankly.

So don't treat all my best gifts with suspicion
forget the fears you took on at the font.
Morality is only superstition.
So why go on refusing what you want?

Ballad of Surprising Turnups

It's something people have to learn ...
Since nothing in this world of ours is certain,
You needn't treat the future with respect.
You really can't predict what's going to happen,
by using laws of cause and their effect.
In this pursuit astrologers and journalists
waste all their words of wisdom and analysis.
They never know which way the coin will turn.

Walking by the Berlin Wall
ten years ago, machine guns placed
where they could kill:
nobody thought, nobody guessed
that it would fall.
Now what comes next?
No one can tell.

A writer sat in prison then.
Committees worked to set him free
from his oppressive government:
nobody thought, nobody guessed,
he would become a President.
Now what comes next?
Let's wait and see.

And that black leader, held
in gaol for thirty years
to keep the peace:
Who would have thought
he'd be released?
And what comes next?
No one suspects.

And those today, who
wash up cups
and take abuse
for all you know, for all you guess
may find some use
for energy,
which sets them free.

As William Fosters, trodden
down at work and home
is given a chance:
for the first time
of all he wants.
How will he be?
We're going to see.

It's something people have to learn …
Since nothing in this world of ours is certain,
You cannot treat the future with respect
You really can't predict what's going to happen,
by using laws of cause and their effect.
In this pursuit, astrologers and journalists
waste all their words of wisdom and analysis.
They never know which way the coin will turn.

Daylight

Homesickness

in memory of Maria Fadeyeva Enzensberger

Yesterday I found a postcard with your scrawl:
'Darling, we are all horses, how is it
you haven't learned that yet?' And at once
your high-boned, white face rose
beside me like a reproach

as if I had begun to forget the wildness
in the gutturals of your laugh, and
the loneliness of *tosca po rodine*
in the frozen sea of your eyes. But I have not.
You were always my Russia:

the voice of Marina's poetry. We saw you last
in a Moscow of brown streets, puddles, and
people queuing for ice cream: an autumn of anomalies,
women turning back tanks, in St Petersburg
there were teenage boys playing *Deutschland uber alles.*

Your mother, the poet Aliger, brought us into
Sologub's yellow mansion where Ivan found himself
in his underpants and writers fix their *dachas:*
Bulgakov would have enjoyed the chicken livers in coriander.
That day you were shaking with the euphoria

of street victory, as if you had come home
after the bleakness that took you into
Highgate hospital. 'I have been so *frightened,*'
you whispered to me there and I had no answer,
any more than at your table in the Cambridge fens

rich with forest mushrooms, peppers and white cheese,
when you struck the glass to command some speech
of love and closeness, and we all failed you. In London
you found another silence, and now we're only left with
a little honey and sun from Mandelstam's dead bees.

Little Venice

for David

Sunlight on the canal, seagulls and a few boats
low in the water: this street is no longer
your territory but as I drive through,
the cool remembered glitter conjures you:
that note of surprise in your voice
as you tell me of some disaster, your
shoulders shaking in those soft blue
Hemingway roll necks. It was your charm
to have the world become a Truffaut film,
or a Brassens song, in the shared laughter.

'Too clever for your own good,' your Cambridge tutor
said, annoyed to have you bypass steady work
in phrasing essays with a casual wit.
I can't remember who it was you hit,
or why the story passed into your legend,
with Paris, Vietnam, and those Insight bylines
which were a part of the same dangerous glamour,
though underneath you were
always lonely in a childhood anger
women never quite escaped.

You startled me on the telephone yesterday
speaking of a dead friend: '*We both loved you.
You must have known that.*' What I knew
was the way we lived in one another's
imagination, rather as people in the novels
of Malcolm Lowry. Closer companions
coped with daily behaviour. All the same,
your words reached through an unhappy
morning to restore my stamina.

Tony

It was February in Provence and the local market
sold goats' cheese wrapped in chestnut leaves and
thick, painted pottery. The stalls of dark check shirts
were the kind you used to wear, and we began to see you:
burly, bearded, handsome as Holbein's Wyatt,
looking into the eyes of a girl or
jumping up from the brasserie table
to buy truffles from a street vendor.

We stayed with our children like gypsies in a barn
of your wife's family house near Aix, and you fed us
beef *daube*, thrush pâté and wine. Long ago
we sat through the night as a threesome writing
those film reviews I always drove to Heffers
in the early rainlight of a Cambridge morning. We still own
the pearwood Dolmetsch bought at your urging,
and copies of that magazine you and I ran together

which the police came to investigate after
a delivery of *Naked Lunch* from Olympia.
For a few years, you moved whenever we did,
from Adams Road to Sherlock, then De Freville
where the printer we owed money lived next door.
You wrote your first book for three hours a day
and then felt restless, since your body liked
to use its energies and you could lift a car.

Your hair was thick and brown
even in York District Hospital where you murmured
'I'm not dying, am I?' and described
the wild animals calmed with a click in your throat.
We guessed you could withstand a February *mistral*
that gets under the clothes so bitterly down here
more easily than we can, being younger
and more robust though, strangely, no longer alive.

Postcard from the Sporades

You know so much about islands.
Here we are woken by cocks and donkeys.
Village women pick thyme and fennel
below our stone terrace: the air
is heavy with a sweet-smelling citrus.

In Waterstones, I watched you listening
to an Irish Poet, your mouth invisible,
the glamour of sadness in your bearing: a
scholar Garbo. We are reading your book now,
here on an island of shepherds and pirates.

Insomnia

The moon woke me, the pocked and chalky moon
that floods the garden with its silvery blue

and cuts the shadow of one leafy branch across
this bed of ours as if on to bright snow.

The sky is empty. Street lights and stars
are all extinguished. Still the moon flows in,

drowning old landmarks in a magic lake,
the chilly waters lapping at my pillow,

their spell relentless as this cold
unhappiness in which I lie awake.

Eclipse

On both sides of the gardens the tall
houses have put out their lights.
Now the cypress is blue and furry,
night creatures move quietly in the long grass,
and, as if in the ages before electricity,

the moon is a white lantern over the birch trees.
Grandchildren, indulged after the Passover seder,
have stopped using the mouse on my apple mac
to stare through the window at the luminous ball
like primitive people in a world of miracles.

This year, Katriona read the questions from the Haggadah;
Lara knew the ancient stories. Now three generations
sit together, imagining ourselves on the globe
of the earth, and trying to believe it is our own
brown shadow moving over the moon.

Izzy's Daughter

'You must be Izzy's daughter,' they said.
I was a liquid, black stare. An olive face.

'So thin. Doesn't she eat? She reads too much.'
My teasing, brawny aunts upset my mother.

I wanted to be as reckless as a man,
to dive through rough, grey waves on Southport sands,

and shake the salt out of my hair as he did.
Instead, I shivered, blue with cold, on the shore.

But I was Maggie Tulliver, proud of my cleverness,
when the whole family listened to my stories.

He listened, too; troubled, his lips moving,
and dog-brown eyes following every word.

'Where does it all come from?' they marvelled at me.
My timid mother smiled from her quiet corner.

A Glass of Wine

for Emma

In your dream, T.S. Eliot and a chestnut stallion
were being bundled into a taxi, the Old Possum
spectacled, a little furtive, the glowing animal
submissive, both dismissed together
as if from your own life. A fiction,

old friend: your spirit is the living stuff
of poetry. That first winter in Wiltshire,
when the frosty leaves crackled under
our feet, we walked beneath black trees
talking of magic and insanity,

and many times since then you've conjured
poems from sad thoughts, and with your laughter
taught me the way to shrink snubs and disasters
into absurdity, with the black wit
once labelled melancholy 'male as cricket'.

Some people shed friendships as they age
and become the family they thought they'd left behind
(*stetl* traders in my case, as for yours
the fashionable world came through your doors)
but we are speaking now of heart and mind;

I love your Scottish stride and sailing carriage,
yet if we lift a glass of wine at 192,
it is the inner fire still burns in you
I see and quietly salute:
indomitable wildness.

The Convalescent

A painting by Gwen John

'I may be timid, but I am never humble,' she said.
The girl she paints is alone in a cane chair.

Her blue dress gives no hint of the body beneath,
the pinks and browns on the lids of her eyes

are those of the cup and teapot. In this space,
the gaze of a lover has no importance.

The artist was often ill; she neglected herself.
Like her sitter, she was young and much too thin

when Rodin seduced her by candlelight that
first day as his model. He found it hard thereafter

to match her passion. 'Stars in the sky console me,'
she wrote, and the energy of lust went into her work.

This is her painting of another woman. It signals
a recovery from more than influenza.

Lazarus' Sister

On hot nights now, in the smell of trees and water,
you beg me to listen and your words enter my spirit.

Your descriptions unmake me; I am like wood
that thought has wormed; even the angels

that report our innermost wish must be kinder.
And yet, when your face is grey in the pillow, I wake you

gently, kissing your eyes, my need for you
stronger than the hope of love. I carry your body

where the hillside flickers: olive cypress ash.
But nothing brings relief. All our days

are numbered in a book. I try to imagine
a way our story can end without a magician.

Lisson Grove

It is hot July, and sycamore wings lodge
in the windscreen wipers. In your illness,
you are begging me to make sense of your life,

and I am helpless as the single electric fan
whirring in the heat of your room
in the Charter Nightingale hospital.

At your bedside, I feel like someone
who has escaped too lightly
from the great hell of the camps,

except that I don't altogether escape,
when I open the door to the street:
the air is cooler, the sky night blue,

my shoes knock lonely notes from the pavement,
and two tramps salute my return to the car
with ironic cheers and cans of Special Brew.

Separations

There's a whir of wood pigeons this morning:
I should close the study window. Last Spring
two of them tried to build their nest in the music;
big, stubborn birds you had to shift with a broom,
and as the pages fell to the floor I remembered
the scattered papers in that rented room,

when I stayed with you the first time, and how
deeply we overslept, as if in finding each other
our dreams had joined at once in a single stream,
so we could escape the ordinary world, and
make common cause together like comrades
at the end of Clair's *A nous la liberté*.

Ungainly, unworldly creatures we were,
two playing cards precariously leaning
and propping each other up, a friend observed.
But conversation was what you wanted,
some exchange of thought, while I
needed tenderness more than talk.

And so things often went wrong.
We were happy enough exploring the red-light
district in Lille with a lonely Belgian crook, or taking
vodka and pilchards in a house of refuseniks
but at home both of us turned away. You
played music upstairs, I lived in my own song

or on the phone. Now, I've closed the study window.
This morning the sky is pale blue in the birch tree
and you lie asleep, your mouth hurt by last
night's squabble. Will we never escape
the need to sift through the long past together
in our effort to establish a new shape?

Bonds

There are owls in the garden and a dog barking.
After so many fevers and such loss,
I am holding you in my arms tonight, as if
your whole story were happening at once:
the eager child in lonely evacuation
waking into intelligence and then
manhood when we were first *copains*,
setting up tent in a rainy Cornish field, or
hitchhiking down to Marseilles together.

You were braver than I was and so
at your side I was never afraid, looking for
Dom 99 in the snows of suburban Moscow,
or carrying letters through Hungarian customs,
I learnt to trust your intuitions more than my own,
because you could meet Nobel laureates,
tramps and smugglers with the same confidence,
and your hunches worked, those molecular puzzles,
that filled the house with clay and wire models.

In the bad times, when like poor Tom Bowling,
you felt yourself gone for ever more,
and threw away all you deserved, you asked me
What was it all for? And I had no answer, then
or a long time after that madness;
nor can I now suggest new happiness,
or hope of good fortune, other than
staying alive. But I know that lying at your side
I could enter the dark bed of silence like a bride.

Muse

Dissolute, undressed, indoors, we argue
about the old days, how once there was
a time for such pursuits

and how the tender words were spiced
with garlic and rosemary, like
the flesh of a young lamb.

– Is poetry something between
cookery and sacrifice? I murmur
as we pack the goods for market.

– Be quiet. Look. The beech trees are golden,
the air has autumn in it, and the street
lies rain-washed and clean in October sun.

Birdwatching

The birds are returning in May, the curlews and sandpipers,
the kittiwake foraging by the harbour; and two
white headed gulls are setting up together
across the street from our Tromso balcony.
Already they are bonded, they mew to one another;

as one swoops off, the other stretches above the chimney
to look for his return. They caress each other's
plumage with their beaks. We learn they should make
their nest near a lake which this year is still frozen.
Sometimes, we are told, gulls miss the chance to breed,

sometimes they nest in chimneys. We are told the young birds
are clumsy and unruly, learn to fly slowly,
grow larger than parents who remain patient
and bewildered. As the days pass, we grow worried for them.
We take turns watching through binoculars.

In Tromso, seagull eggs, eaten with local beer
are served cut open like an avocado, the thin
shell pale green and mottled. Friends assure us
the gull population rises every year nevertheless.
But I am squeamish about lifting the yolk to my lips.

Picnic

for Roy Tommy Eriksen

Here on the far side of Whale island
where the water is bottleglass blue,
we are having a picnic. There's a dazzle
of sunshine on snow, and around us
mountains cut sharp as crystal.

We are 70 degrees North, but
the landscape is warmed by the drift
of Caribbean waters, and this is
May, the dark time is past
in the Norwegian Arctic.

These are the seas of Greenland halibut,
and catfish with teeth and tongue, yet
it is a gentle Renaissance scholar
who makes a bonfire between stones,
and hangs a kettle on a found stick.

His red-haired wife laughs over
sizzling meat. But what I remember
is how on the way home the same friend
ignored a painful back to climb over the edge
of a cliff to rescue your lost denture.

After the Arctic

Flew South, still drugged with white sunshine,
dry-skinned, already used to a few streets
between snow slopes, painted wooden
homes, mountains in every window.
We found fresh leaves on birch trees,

damp green of the first chestnut,
yellow blossom, all the tenderness
of English spring. And the next morning
we woke to birdsong, but were ill-tempered,
as if denied an accustomed euphoriant.

Wheelchair

We've travelled on a bumboat on the green South China seas,
seen papaya, dates and coconuts in crotches of the trees
and in Hawker centres Singapore keep quietly policed
eaten hundred year old eggs and fishbrains wrapped in bamboo leaf.
We've seen coolies who sold goats milk and the men who
                                            plundered them
while the ghosts of Maugham and Coward haunt the new Raffles
                                                        hotel;

but the most surprising feature of the perils we have passed
is you've travelled in a wheelchair with your left leg in a cast.
Most people would have had more sense, but we were both surprised
to find it rather soothing. And one day we surmised:
you needed an attention that I hardly ever pay
while I enjoyed the knowledge that you couldn't get away.

Now the generator flickers far inland in Campuhan
and we lie inside our cottage cooled remotely by a fan,
or take a bath among the ferns and tall hibiscus trees.
Green rice grows in the paddy fields, we pick the coffee beans.
And outside, parked and ready, sits the chair that takes you round
to explore in a contentment that we've only rarely found.

Dead Writers

In Pushkin's house, it is all as it was
when he went out to duel with d'Anthès:
his wife's elegant needlework, the household bills.

Akhmatova's single room now holds
a golden chair, her oak desk and her bed;
all is tidiness, where once there was disorder.

Russia treasures her poets, once they're dead.
In England, we depend on one another:
the trees my friend planted, grown to a forest,

the white lace bed once offered for my solace.
The river at his garden end flows cold and fast.
Stories, suffering, poetry. All as it was.

The White Bird

for Anna Akhmatova

How marvellously you squandered yourself,
Anna Andreevna, your Tatar bearing
royal in a casual shawl, and wearing
a ring that was a gift of the moon.

Always a witch not a wife, in the house
of three husbands your most
adulterous love was for
the poems they didn't want written

and you could never abandon.
Even as the gay sinner of Tsarskoye Selo,
the future cast its shadow into your heart.
Tonight, I drink to your ruined house,

loneliness, and that white bird
you chose instead of happiness.

Fyodor: Three Lyrics

1

In Bad Homburg, I watched him over the tables,
the homely face, false teeth, poor clothes.
I'm a Swiss doctor, but I read novels.

When he had lost every coin from his worn purse
he looked up at me and smiled:
'I am a man,' he said, 'without a future.'

I had treated him the night before
for epilepsy, and he spoke then of
the joy he felt while lying on the floor

one moment before the foam and spasms.
His face was shining there as he explained:
'Christ alone,' he said, 'can save Russia.'

2

In Basel, the church floats in the moon
and the trees whiten. There is no casino.
I met him once again with his new wife,

looking at Holbein's coffined Christ,
that decomposing body, green and blue,
the swollen limbs like ripened gooseberries.

He turned, and though he did not recognise
my face, answered my greeting so:
'I shall burn everything I once worshipped.'

What were his sins, then, more than recklessness,
disorder, and a young wife's jewels pawned?
I sometimes wonder if perhaps his genius

(so foreign to this sober, cobbled city
piled above gorges where the black Rhine flows)
had in the very sob of its own pity

another throb of cruelty and pleasure
that made the writing shimmer. Well, I know
I do more human good here as a doctor.

Exile

for Joseph Brodsky

Once you gave me New York.
You led me under a bridge to look
from a wasteland of broken bottle
and beer-can up at the mirror glass
boat of Manhattan. I don't know why
you never went back to your baroque

pale-green city, with the grey Neva
flowing down to the Baltic, but then,
we've not been close, Joseph, though
it happened I was with you when
twenty years ago, you heard
about that first bypass, and so

can remember you talking, as if to yourself,
imagining what it meant to be dead,
with an ironic slant to your face,
and the love of pleasure in your full under-lip
as you nodded up at an untidy bookshelf.
'After that, there is only the book,' you said.

Companionship

It was Wordsworth's clear line I wanted,
nothing to do with mountains, only the quiet
sunshine and silence, but I hated being alone.
The lonely cannot love solitude.

I wanted a garden outside tall windows,
winter sun in leafless branches, a cold spring
with crocus in the grass and the first blossom.
and you at work in the same apartment,

my dearest friend. Today I was watching
a grey squirrel fly in the beech trees when
your words reached into me: 'You know,
a poet isn't much of a companion.'

Wigmore Hall

for Martin

In July heat, beneath the frieze of blue where
golden Apollo stands beneath muse and scribe,
the four musicians have removed their jackets;
and in red braces, silver flute in hand,
you pause to smile, and wipe your misted glasses.

Long ago, when you were at school in
Grantchester Meadows, one speech day
in a hot school hall, your hair too long,
untidy, you came on at eight years old,
after the madrigals to play a folk song,

and the sleepy audience of bored
parents and fellow pupils waiting for
the distribution of prizes, slowly began to attend
and burst into applause when the song ended.
You were surprised, and a shy smile

transformed your face. Let's hope
tonight there's no Apollo to be envious
of these notes singing out in curving line,
as you risk putting yourself to the test
rather than dream 'I might have been' from a desk.

Staking Tomatoes

for Adam

The leaves of four droopy tomato plants
release tobacco harshness, as your fingers
that know their way through Chopin on the piano,
try clumsily to tie these stems to a fence.
Neither of us are natural gardeners.

Long ago in the moonlight of Trumpington
we stayed up feeding roots and spraying
leaf curl in the peach tree. You were gallant,
a poet at ten years old, your smile open,
loyally unheeding my neglect.

There are Belmondo lines of laughter now,
while your two daughters watch with admiration.
But those tomatoes grew red and plump,
as it turns out: undeserved gifts,
like stories from your newly fluent pen.

Birthday

for Joel

My golden-eyed and tender-hearted son,
when you were young, you were too gentle even
to kill a spider in the bath, and when

a terrapin escaped its tank and lived
one stubborn month behind a radiator,
its silly courage touched you into tears.

Being so hurt by other creatures' pain,
you grew up slowly. High on home-made
stilts you stomped between the next-door children

like a giant of whom no one was afraid.
And then you lived in Dalkey where the white houses
dazzle and the morning sky falls into

the long blue puddles left by the sea.
The small birds pecked up prawns, or rose
in flocks, while you observed their beauty.

When you pick up your violin to play
these days, music still makes you happy.
What else you want, you can't be brought to say.

Bed

for a grandchild at six months

The summer garden breathes through my
window, baby Natasha. Untroubled on a pillow,
your eyelids in the rapid movement of dreams, you
learn the scent of my skin and hair,
the body warmth of this bed.

And what I'd wish you to inherit is
the sense of your pretty mother and
your father's brave heart, and grow to relish
the ordinary privilege of daylight
in their house of music and easy laughter.

Now let these words be a loving charm
against the fear of loneliness, and
under a cold moon, you may remember
this bundled duvet as somewhere once
familiar, where you came to no harm.

Amy Levy

Precocious, gifted girl, my nineteenth-century
voice of Xanthippe, I dreamed of you last night,
walking by the willows behind the Wren,
and singing to me of Cambridge and unhappiness.

'Listen, I am the first of my kind, and
not without friends or recognition,
but my name belongs with my family
in Bayswater, where the ghosts

of wealthy Sephardim line the walls,
and there I am alien because I sing.
Here, it is my name that makes me strange.
A hundred years on, is it still the same?'

The First Wriggle

Going to buy milk from the corner shop
on a Tuesday in August with the warm rain
tasting of roses, I suddenly felt an illicit
moment of good fortune: a freedom

in which poems could happen.
It's rather like the grander forms of creation.
Worms on Mars should surprise nobody;
life will form, wherever there's opportunity.

Miracles

After reading Richard Dawkins

Let us consider the dance between fig and wasp,
how the fruit is a flower garden, and the wings
of the female insect are torn off upon entering;
that she lays her eggs in the sweetness of the flesh,
and her grubs bear pollen to fertilise the tree.

You explain that the insect must not use all
the flowers in the fig, or the tree will have no seed,
so there are systems that police her greed,
the simplest, that too many eggs lead the fruit
to drop, so that all her grubs die,

which is an evolution both ruthless and accurate:
the unguided cleverness at work on this planet.

White Flowers

Why should I feel a ripple of apprehension
receiving a gift of white flowers in February,
daisies and carnations, delivered to my door
in florist tissue and white ribbon? It's because
my mother wouldn't have them in the house,
before the Spring solstice. However,

I've put them in a stoneware jar. I'm not
much given to acts of defiance, always had
trouble throwing off superstition:
as a child I counted birds, and believed
in lucky numbers. A necklace
I remember of Russian amber

with stones like lions' teeth had to be worn
even to fetch the post in the worst years;
but I don't hold with my own cowardice
so I display these flowers now without
flamboyance, but with resolution:
a gesture in the name of divine reason.

Rumanian Candle

For all the stench of Bucharest car exhaust
with snow in my lashes and eight year old boys
at my sleeve, who couldn't be chased away,
nagging, '*I love you, pretty lady,*
give me five hundred lei,'

what reached me in my fatigue was a light
in the faces of people who love poetry.
Over frozen white fields, where neglected
villages collapse like broken outhouses,
or in the Hapsburg rococo

of Oradea, where talk slithered uneasily
over the last years of the war
I could make out the same glow:
it was like a candle behind the skin
of their lit faces.

Gorilla

London in August, watching
Hancock repeats. His was a very English
genius: that dingy bedsitter with its floral
fifties prints, the bakelite wireless set;
his putty face miming schoolboy
vanity and gloating. His death saddened
us, but shouldn't have surprised.

What he mocked was the rashness
of unprivileged aspiration, and we laughed
at such a prisoning lack of hope, as if
we were outside the bars looking in
at the great sad figure of a gorilla,
one leather prehensile thumb on
the ball of his jaw. Only we weren't
outside, we were caught in the same system.

Greek Gender

As we learn the new alphabet, a woman is bent
over a pail of paint, white-washing her doorstep.

When we look back along the narrow street, another
woman dressed in black is passing, laden with potatoes.

At the next table, three handsome men in shirtsleeves
sit quietly drinking coffee. We grasp the pronouns,

even the awkward neuters. Above us,
the male tree of a pair of figs is heavy with false fruit.

Holidays

Here on the terrace by the donkey path
we watch old women picking wild spinach.
There are goats to be milked, and cheese to be made.
In Greece, human work has its simplicities.

Holiday makers have to make their own rhythms,
which are not so easy to find: sleep
in the afternoon, swimming in the late sun.
And thinking about the work we left behind.

Visiting Hospital

Walking through so many wards to look for you
surrounded by books and papers, wide awake

and wanting to talk, I pass those other patients
snoring in their beds and must remember

Larkin's old fools and what we shall all find out.
Now I would guess we see only the tether

of sleepers who leave nurses and treatment behind
to dream of their own childhood more often than dying.

Their teeth grin in a glass; their silence breathes.
Even in their depleted lives, they do not feel completed.

Haverstock Hill

It is a cold March day, and
a leafless tree is singing fiercely:
the bird, if there is a bird, invisible,
the voice of mating and territory
rising from dry boughs in vegetable
and ventriloquist urgency.

It is an accident of a shift in the axis
of the fuming earth, but I am listening
to life drawn from town soil, and
the radiance of pale sunlight, as if
to a song of wood that has not been
altogether exhausted by winter.

Mother

My mother wore tweed suits and court shoes.
When she came to school, my form teacher
found her a perfect lady and told me henceforth
my wild behaviour wouldn't be excused.

'If you came from a slum it would be different.'
She didn't know her words filled me with glee.
I hated the thought of turning into someone who
carried gloves and couldn't drive a car and I didn't want

to make fine pastry or keep the linen in order.
'Woman,' my father said, 'where is my dinner?'
It was his joke to pretend that mastery
though altogether he depended on her

while she, like her unmarried brother and sister,
could have lived quite cheerfully as a spinster.
I was too afraid of inheriting her colon
cancer and her stoic mildness

to copy her ways, or even to see how
much her tender courage gave to me
a stubborn daughter keeping my own stall
earning a livelihood by telling stories.

Old Movies

At fifteen, in a Torquay cinema
Bacall and Bogart dazed me
with a flash of sexual recognition:
the electricity of their grand adventure
was worth more than a whole comfortable life.

My parents were perplexed.
Years later, I wept in the rain
of a Leicester cemetery and
remembered their quiet happiness.
Now I know: it's love we crave not sex.

Allegiance

We like to eat looking at boats. At night
in Jaffa harbour, the whole sea is alight
with glow worms of the local fisherman's floats.

My English friend has blue flirtatious eyes
and feels no danger. Her intrepid forbears
first explored, then colonized the planet.

Now over Yemenite eggplant and fried dough
we talk about the Roman exploitation
of Caesarea two thousand years ago

and find the history easy to agree.
Politics here and now are another matter.
The scared, open faces of the soldiers

look like oppressors to her, while my inheritance
– Kovno, Odessa, packing and running away –
makes me fear for them, as if they were sons.

So I can't share the privilege of guilt. Nor could
she taste the Hebrew of Adam in
the red earth here: the iron, salt and blood.

Ninety Two

If he was listening he made no sign,
my uncle in his Blundell Sands nursing home.
Under the tight bedclothes I could see
his limbs were skinny as a grasshopper's;
there was even a frictional insect noise
from time to time as he rubbed dry hands together.
I began giving him family news, and was soon apologising
for leaving him up North in his comfortable prison

so I could get on with my own living.
He said nothing, until I mentioned a son
who didn't want to marry, then he murmured
'I never did either' with sudden clarity.
I decided my casual thought was
the first to enter his inner world, because
the rest of my gossip had no relevance

to the story he was moving through.
I was ashamed of my own egotism.
He was engaged once. When that went wrong
he lived alone, played golf, and though
girls liked him, lived a bachelor. 'Was there
no one else then?' I asked him curiously.
In the long pause, I watched him try to remember.

Morden Tower

Went North last week, to read at Morden Tower
after thirty years: do you remember
that 'Stray Dog' of a generation far
from Petersburg, and without Akhmatova,

of Harwood and Raworth, Fisher and Crozier,
Ginsberg on tour, and Basil Bunting?
Behind the same postern door, up
stone steps from Back Stowell Street,

the hipster North waited. I was in something
shiny and Japanese, my long hair loose,
my nerves twitching. Later,
when I crossed two fields in a gale

to the shepherd's hut where Tom Pickard
lived with his red-haired Connie, I was still
too scared to eat their sorrel soup. They saw me
as someone from the squeamish South,

but I was no more comfortable in Cambridge
than I am now a part of the new age.
Poets don't fit. Never have. I guess
we'll just have to trust the words on the page.

Rosemary in Provence

We stopped the Citroen at the turn of the lane,
because you wanted a sprig of blue rosemary
to take home, and your coat opened awkwardly

as you bent over. Any stranger would have
seen your frail shoulders, the illness
in your skin – our holiday on the Luberon

ending with salmonella –
but what hurt me, as you chose slowly,
was the delicacy of your gesture:

the curious child, loving blossom
and mosses, still eager
in your disguise as an old man.

Party Time

It's lovely in the bathroom:
green marble floor, cool tiles
and trailing plants. Sometimes
I can't think why anybody wants
to plod around a room explaining
who they are and what they care about.
In here I am quite happy alone
with my own thought.

After a time, though, and long before
that urgent knock on the door, I remember
how, when things have gone most
seriously wrong, a group of people
no more intimate than this
have sometimes had the power to restore
a sense of who I am. It's lovely
in the bathroom nevertheless:
but not for long.

Mirror

Mirror, mirror, what's going on?
A matron aunt or stubborn father
these days looks out of the mirror.
When I smile at them they are gone.

A pace behind the silvered glass
they wait like ghosts, though not so much
scary as shy, eager to touch
my present flesh with their own past.

Within my body is a thread
of which resemblance is the sign:
my story is not only mine
but an extension of the dead.

Prayer

The windows are black tonight. The lamp
at my bedside peering with its yellow
40 watt light can hardly make out the chair.
Nothing is stranger than the habit of prayer.

The face of God as seen on this planet
is rarely gentle: the young gazelle is food
for the predator; filmy shapes
that need little more than carbon and water,

evolve like patterns on Dawkins'
computer; the intricate miracles
of eye and wing respond to the same
logic. I accept the evidence.

God is the wish to live. Everywhere,
as carnivores lick their young with
tenderness, in the human struggle
nothing is stranger than the habit of prayer.

Gold

Gold

1

A wintry gold floods the bedroom this morning:
a January sun, drenching the air, alight
in a silk scarf, a yellow flare in the mirror.
I used to revel in the glitter of night,
but, over here, the dark has little glamour.

Let me introduce myself: Lorenzo da Ponte.
Mozart would smile to see me here in America
weighing out tea or measuring a yard
of plug tobacco. I have bolts of cloth,
salt pork in kegs, sewing thread, waxed cord.

My customers are cobblers or carters.
They offer lame horses and watery cider
instead of money; I must be content
to scratch a meagre living as a grocer.
It is a mask I wear, and I have spent

most of my life in one disguise or another.
Living on my wits – *Se vuol ballare,*
Signor Contino – like my Figaro,
but always more of an interloper.
Where did I find the nerve to put my toe

over the baroque threshold of the feudal?
My father lived in the stink of untreated
leather, without comfort or property,
hoping for nothing more than our survival.
He knew nothing of Tasso or Dante.

And so was spared the evil whispers
behind the jewelled hands of gorgeous
ladies in the Imperial Court.
In Europe, the children of tanners
do well to remain tanners.

2

I remember three Empires, but
what do I recall by now of Ceneda?
Disorder, hunger, urine, cats in
the streets and all the usual clobber
of poverty, shoeless children, dirt.

If there were any men with fat purses
in that ghetto north of Venice, my father
was not among them, poor man, confused
by many creditors, he was no usurer,
but rather harshly used.

Ceneda put a sibilance in my Italian,
although I never learnt the stoop of
the older generation, and women,
I soon noticed, like my courteous
words, fine hands, and even

the stranger's darkness in my eyes.
D'ove sono i bei momenti. Yes,
lovely creatures, ill used by their husbands,
were generous to me. You hear their voice
in my sad aria for the Countess,

Mozart transfigured in his garden music.
D'ove sono i bei momenti? My pen
could race down pages, lickety-split,
writing of the unhappiness in women.
You will not find my words in Beaumarchais.

Here in Elizabethville, a girl with skin
of white milk and dimples, often
comes into my shop with a child
to collect her husband's medicine.
I know he bullies her. One day,

I saw a bruise under her eye. Before
my lips had framed the obvious question
her boy surprised me – *Mister, what happened
to your teeth?* She pulled him close
to hush him in his ear. I am a man

in late middle age, a little vain – toothless
or not – and scrupulously dressed.
I still walk upright, though I use a cane.
And briefly, I was tempted to confess
the flattering details of a scabrous story.

My Nancy was upstairs, however, making
her *capelletti Bolognese.* So,
for all my rumoured immorality, not a
tender word was spoken, though
she might have listened like a Desdemona,

and perhaps my snubs and humiliations
would then have gained the spell of an adventure,
as if I had chosen to live on the run.
Just as the very dust of the air in
sunshine takes on the lustre of sequins.

3

The teeth? Well, I'll come to that story later.
There's a more serious matter, which still grates
in my flesh like seeds of dirt in an oyster.
I wanted to live with a bit of flash and brio,
rather than huddle behind ghetto gates.

It's not a question of faith. What I wanted to do
I knew as soon as I started to read Italian,
learnt on my own from torn books in the attic.
And only poetry could work the magic
of changing me into a European.

My mother died before I was five. My father,
too distressed to comfort anyone, found teachers
who were ignorant of Latin. I was not content
to be excluded from the opportunity of
being a child of the Enlightenment.

Far from getting answers to my questions,
my brother and I were often whipped.
As for scruples of my ancient religion,
I learnt little of those beyond the script
of the Hebrew language, though

a few sayings entered my imagination.
If I am not for myself, as Hillel has it,
who will be for me? And if I am
only for myself, what am I? And if
not now, when? He was a poet.

When I was fourteen, my father wished
to marry a Christian girl. The price
was the conversion of the whole family.
Knowing so little of what I was to enter,
I thought Christendom must be Paradise.

There were drums beating, cathedral bells,
halberdiers in ceremonial dress, the Feast
of the beheading of St John the Baptist,
when I who was born Emanuele
Conigliano became Lorenzo da Ponte.

I knelt down to become a citizen, and
shoved my origins out of my mind. I thought
if a little water purified my hand,
my spirit could flow into the main stream,
whatever earlier generations taught.

It seemed a gift of fortune unalloyed
when the same Bishop, whose name we'd taken,
put my brother and I in a seminary. Buoyed
up by reading Petrarch, Ovid, Horace,
I became so crazily studious

I had no time to chafe at celibate life.
My mentors, sadly, thought me too ambitious,
and mocked my first verses. Those who find
in my behaviour only desire for material good
miss out my schoolboy trust in all mankind.

4

Venice was water and sky, barges
of musicians on the Grand Canal,
perfumes, fans, a fever of carnival.
On my first visit there, I fell in love
with the whole city: the shops open,

till midnight, shopkeepers singing
as loudly as gondoliers. I lingered
in bookshops and in coffee houses
talking to men of letters. On my first visit,
I won the reputation of a wit.

The next, I had my purse of coins stolen
and didn't care, since I could see beggars
able to relish singers and lanterns.
Alas, I was to blame in staying on, for
when my father's leather shop went under,

he'd urged my brother and I into the Church
to train as priests – and I did not resist.
For someone of my temperament, that mask
was one, at least, that should have been rejected.
A priestly vow is dangerous, if neglected.

To begin with, venal sins aroused little
opprobrium as such. How I behaved
with girls was altogether commonplace.
Voi che sapete ... I was soon the slave
of Angiola, a ferocious beauty

who taught me all that was depraved
in pleasure, praising my precocity,
with delicate caresses, smiling to see
anxieties forgotten. She encouraged me
to think a little money might

keep our delicious nights alive for ever.
My friend Casanova, who was much colder,
more brutal – he devoured women like
sweetmeats – warned me her brother
was a well-known pimp but I took no notice

– Venice was a city of courtesans – though
sometimes glances that the two exchanged
held an affection something more than sibling.
I was too young, and did not want to know
what in the outcome had me half deranged.

So I joined their gambling in taverns.
Once a good hearted gondolier lent
me a few coins, and that won others, so
for a time I became Angiola's mascot.
The gift I gave back. And the rest we spent.

Now where, I wonder, did that fiction rise
that all my tribe are both wealthy and mean?
When on the Rialto, sometimes, I saw men
in beards wearing their gaberdines,
with sallow faces, I lowered my eyes,

in case they read my stare as one that mocked.
They were old, and sad, and if there lurked
among them any single, vengeful Shylock,
he would not cherish any hope of justice
within the noble Christian courts of Venice.

Infatuated, dissolute, poor, at last
I tried on a new mask; that of magician.
And since Venetians put some trust
in alchemy, for a time I prospered,
as if I were a licensed conjuror,

though naturally no gold was ever made.
The Church still took no interest in me.
It was as if I'd simply found a trade.
The role was one I might even have played
for longer, if one afternoon I had not

found my sweet Angiola in our bed
with two men, entertained lasciviously.
Challenged, she threw an inkpot at my head.
I had no choice. I picked up a few clothes.
That very hour, without much dignity

I left the city in a jealous temper,
making for Treviso, where I could
earn some money as a Latin teacher,
while writing a few poems on the need
for human beings to behave as brothers.

My politics at the time were innocent.
I did not imagine much original
in what I wrote, almost as exercise.
The morals I approved were Roman, decent;
but looked seditious to an Abbot's eyes.

And I was in the Church. All of my past
actions were examined in a new light.
I stood accused as gambler, fornicator,
adulterer and rapist, though that last
for my own pride I must deny.

Those poems brought me to the attention
of the Venetian Senate. The Inquisition
was soon investigating my conversion.
I did not stay to argue the position,
but left sweet Venice quickly for Trieste.

5

And what to do next? My brother's income
was, I well knew, committed to support
my father and the family. From now on,
the Church banned my employment as teacher.
Was I condemned to living as a con man?

Not my intention, but I'd have to busk it.
I was outside Venetian jurisdiction, but
the Church has a long arm, as well I knew,
and even to earn my bread I dared not risk it.
You cannot always recognise

the good news from the bad. I might,
without that incident, have spent
my whole life in a dingy backwater.
Instead, it was to Dresden that I went
to see an old friend, who was Court poet

to the opera. He knew I had some talent,
though while I hung around he did
little to further it. It was only
the morning I was on my way
the fellow seemed suddenly to relent,

as if sure then of no awkward demands.
He scribbled a few lines to Salieri
in Vienna: 'Do for him everything
that you would do for me.'
And with that letter a new life began.

6

Enough. You want to hear about Mozart.
How did he live? Who were his favourite women?
Did he have any secret habits, stuff
he put in Tokay, or snorted with his snuff?
As if what genius does for recreation

has much to tell us about what he is.
I can only say: I loved the man,
and if you wonder what I had in common
— apart from laughter and frivolities —
with such a genius, famous since he was six,

I'd say: though I was a late starter
we rapidly gained the same enemies
— Casti, for instance, syphilitic, burring
through the wreckage of his nose —
as both of us hustled on the peripheries.

In Vienna, nothing counts but rank.
A Baron with a house in Herrengasse,
and all his land in hock, still keeps a gig
painted with family insignia, his wig
is well cut, and his clothes elegant.

That's Empire for you. And always, at the centre,
toadies will prosper more than any talent.
Which is not to say I couldn't flatter
but even at the height of my acceptance,
the snobbish flunkeys always had my measure.

Still, there were pretty milliners, dressed
in feathers, cafés on the Graben.
At first, I took up lodging with a tailor
near Taborgasse, where the market stalls
sold trinkets, hot potato cakes, and shawls,

and settled in, before taking my letter
to Salieri in the First District. Naturally
I greeted him at once as an Italian,
while he read over what I'd brought, with caution.
I didn't mention my priestly career,

but said I had a Bishop as a godfather.
On some matters, I had to stay alert,
if not evasive, since the Emperor's mother
in her lifetime had allowed no Jews, convert
or other, place in her Vienna.

Salieri introduced me to the Emperor;
I was appointed to the Italian Theatre,
and on that stage discovered my true home.
The make believe delighted me at once:
I loved the candle starlight, painted domes,

the filmy, shimmering clothes, and feathery wings
which transformed actors into gods and kings.
That said, the only people there who prosper
in opera houses are the leading singers.
They hold the rest to ransom: scene shifters,

tailors, extras, engineers, composers
and poets always bottom of the pile.
Salieri I thought witty and versatile,
but my first opera, let me confess,
– with his music – was not a success.

The Emperor was kind about my failure,
encouraged me to try my luck again;
when the next went well, he whispered
to me: *Abbiamo vinto*. So I was in favour.
For a time, could use green porcelain

to eat my breakfast, sit on lacquered
white chairs with goats' feet, wear
an ankle length coat of Chinese silk,
and be a guest in the Imperial palace,
though I might well fear poison in the chalice.

When I was ill, I warmed my bed with embers
in a copper pan, drank claret and madeira.
I worked for anyone: Martin y Soler,
Martini, Storace. Whoever asked.
I learnt my trade as I performed the task.

Is it a serious art to write libretti
when so few people listen to the words?
Those who found me glib, would often say
I did no more than *translate* poetry,
and steal the shape of better writers' plays.

Beaumarchais himself was rather kinder.
He said *The Marriage of Figaro*, cut
into our version, was a miracle, and that
to turn a five act play into an opera
was of itself to make a new drama.

When Mozart wanted to set *Figaro*, the play
was banned in Austria, I dared suggest
I knew exactly what could be hacked out.
And Emperor Joseph let us have our way.
It was a risk, but somehow I had guessed

that in that chance lay immortality. I changed
Figaro's first name, for superstition:
Beaumarchais had him as Emanuel,
which was my own name before baptism.
I wanted no gossip about my religion

– as if that would ever dwindle away.
There were many around us who were jealous,
not of my skills, of course, but Mozart's genius,
and they included Salieri, my first patron.
It was stupid of me, then, to start a liaison

with a singer that he thought belonged to him.
In those days I was rash, and handsome,
with all my teeth. Ah yes. I promised you
that story. I have never been quite sure
how much what followed had to do with him.

A girl where I lodged had dismissed her lover,
praising my good looks. I hardly knew her,
or the rejected lover, save as a surgeon,
till I met him in a coffee shop, and mentioned
one of my gums might have to be lanced.

'Cut?' he said. 'No need of that.
For a sequin I will rid you of the trouble.'
When he returned he had a blue glass bottle.
'Put this on your gums,' he said, 'with a cloth.'
And so I did, and thanked him for his skill.

My nature at the time was not suspicious.
I was putting on the lotion with a placid
hand, obedient to instructions, without
a thought of any danger, when
my maid screamed out: 'Jesus, that's nitric acid!'

– she often used the stuff for washing clothes.
I did not doubt her, rinsed my mouth at once
with vinegar and milk. The harm was done.
And in a few days my gums were wax.
On the left side my teeth dropped one by one.

7

They didn't take to *Figaro* in Vienna.
We had to wait for Prague. One day,
along the Graben, I met Casanova.
I was feeling low, since hearing that my brother
– abler than me and far more virtuous –

had fallen ill and died. I cursed whatever
powers muddle up God's justice.
My friend and I fell into each other's arms.
Although we'd quarrelled long ago in Venice,
I never wished the fellow any harm.

We dined that evening with a pretty dancer
and La Ferarrese, an opera diva
of whom you will hear more. In Grinzing
we ate roast goose and drank champagne together.
Soon after, I was afire with *Don Giovanni*,

and put the plot of it in front of Mozart.
He liked it, and I've never written faster.
I kept awake by taking Seville snuff,
a girl of sixteen sitting close enough
for me to fondle, when my ink ran dry.

And then it was a tranquil Prague October.
I recall autumn leaves, and birdshell skies;
in an old farmhouse Mozart and Constanze
stayed – I have never heard such birdsong –
while I lodged opposite the three Lions.

We were still doing re-writes that week,
so I was involved in the rehearsals,
but Mozart would not write the overture.
The more we pleaded, the more he was playful.
At last, we tricked him into the Bertramka

and locked him in upstairs with his piano.
Seeing us through the window, he spoke
fretfully of being left alone. We passed up wine
and baked meat, begging him resign
himself to work, and then he took it as a joke,

and with relief we heard the first notes
of the score. A coachman took me home.
That night I walked about the city,
enjoying Prague, and gossiping with Czechs
whose late night badinage was wry and witty.

Their theatre goers favour the dramatic.
They have a legend of an ancient monster
haunting the stones of the Jews' cemetery,
but they are my ghosts, the dead who lie there,
and, if unquiet, they don't frighten me.

It was my touch to have the father's statue
return for his revenge, though Mozart
blenched at it. He felt some guilt, I knew,
for disobedience of his own father. I had
no fear of mine rising out of Hell

since he was still alive and short of money,
no apparition needed to remind.
In *Stavoske Divadlo*, that anxiety
quickly dropped out of my mind. It was
the prettiest Theatre I had seen.

And at the first performances, I gasped
to see the audience in their finery
and hear the bustle; I had never grasped
what listening to applause would mean to me.
I knew they'd loved our *Figaro*, of course,

but had not heard the clapping for myself
or felt elation stirring in my blood. Seeing
my own libretto, bound in gold paper
sold outside at 40 crowns a copy
seemed to authenticate my whole being.

8

The dialogue, the counterpoint, the melodies:
La ci darem la mano was my favourite.
Meanwhile composers, still using my libretti,
began to mock my ignorance of music,
and often said, you cannot trust a man,

who cannot even play a simple piano,
and makes his living out of writing opera.
He speaks too cleverly, and so it is
that foolish women throw themselves at him.
La Ferrarese, say, who played Susanna

in *Marriage of Figaro*, during its revival.
She was my mistress, yes, although
she brought me to my knees more by her
singing than her beauty, her contralto
voice, teasing as well as pleasing.

I knew the substance of her reputation
– her jealousy, her street violence –
but, warned against the association
because she had so many enemies,
I became even more her partisan,

and gave her parts for which she was
unsuited. Meanwhile, many voices
spoke viciously of my collaboration:
in *Cosi fan tutti*. It was a gentle variation
on the old story of inconstant women.

Mozart's angelic harmonies transformed
my wicked plot, but there were moralists
who found me cynical, and warned
I should not be indulged inside the Court.
Salieri arranged most of the slanders.

Perhaps it was support of La Ferrarese
made me so unpopular? Her song
was out of fashion, and she herself was old
when our love ended. Something went wrong.
And soon the new Emperor, Leopold,

looked on me with so much disfavour
I had to leave the comforts of Vienna
for London, marriage and financial ruin.
But let me say, my bride was not the problem.
My Nancy had amazing acumen,

as well as youth and beauty. In my English
troubles – with an unscrupulous producer
whose notes I'd signed in rather foolish
fashion – Nancy was much shrewder.
She ran a coffee house and kept the profit

in her own name, until we sailed away
from Europe, debts and prejudice –
she was another convert, by the way –
to a New World over the stormy seas
where nobody recalls our histories.

9

To speak now as an enlightened ghost,
my end was better than you might suppose.
In New York, in a bookshop once, I met
by chance a man who loved Italian poets.
When he discovered what I knew by heart

he introduced me to his wealthy friends.
And even as Nancy and I entered society,
the Italian Opera with my *Don Giovanni*
was crossing the Atlantic. When it arrived,
I found that my celebrity revived.

My Nancy became a renowned hostess,
who carried herself with grace and, since
she spoke four languages, easily impressed
our new admirers. As for me,
I taught the treasures of Italian poetry.

Poor Mozart was so much less fortunate.
My only sadness is to think of him, a pauper,
lying in his grave, while I became
Professor of Italian literature.
Nobody living can predict their fate.

I moved across the cusp of a new age,
to reach this present hour of privilege.
On this earth, luck is worth more than gold.
Politics, manners, morals all evolve
uncertainly. Best then to be bold.

Living Room

How can we make friends before one of us dies
if you quarrel with two fingers in your ears,
like a child? Things won't come out right now.
You think I don't love you. I won't argue.
Your angry sadness stings me into tears.
I think of your old mac, smelling of chemicals,
leant against long ago in the 'Everyman' queue,

when you offered me those tender early
films that made our lips tremble, or else
the forgiven boy in the forest of Ravel's opera,
more touching to me than your verbal
skills or passion for the genius of gesture
in crayon, mime, *commedia del arte*.
It's love we miss, and cannot bear to lose.

I know you would much prefer I choose
intelligence to prize, but that has
always had its down side, your words
so often cut me down to size, I wonder
if some accident removed me first, whether
my writing days would count as evidence
that in my loss was little real to miss.

The likeliest end is that the bay tree left
to my attention, withers on the window sill,
and moths lay eggs in the lentils, while
still hurt by memories of you as gentle, I'll
look into a monitor for comfort, and cry
aloud at night in the hope somewhere
your lonely spirit might hang on and care.

Still Life

Out of a tale by Washington Irving

After your monstrous sleep, you woke lying
in the doorway of a shop selling bankrupt stock,
with two buskers and a pit bull guarding their tin;
a wintry city, the wind getting up, and ghosts in your head
that no one else remembers. In the window
you make out white bristles pushing through skin.

Bewildered, as if in the fairy tale, your back
sunk against old clothes, you mull over
what became of your life, what you might
have done, or could have, if not for
the spell that held you. Dozing,
you try to remember,

to hear the voice of your own working mind
against the rap of this millennial city,
where the biology of tenderness is forgotten
and the only ties are those of single
electrons forming bonds between
atoms in a craving for stability.

Paradise

Even the sad music from the car radio is glamorous
this morning, as I take the curve up the hill.
The sun glitters on rainy streets
like a shoal of herrings in water,
this early March tingles my blood
as yellow touches the strands of a willow:
a freedom intoxicating and dangerous.

No one knows where I am. No one
cares what I do. It's alarming
to be untethered as a kite slipped from
a child's hand, and then blown past
this high street of shop windows: Monsoon,
French Connection, Waterstones.

The last gives me pause. I wonder
whether it was cowardice or duty
denied me this pleasure so long,
to take comfort from the name on a book spine
or italic under a photo, while the blood
of my life found a pulse only in song.

After La Traviata

She calls *Too late* from her bed, and in fury
I feel the hot salt spilling out of my eyes,
as if her need to love undermined all witness.
One great cry, and we forget his mistrust,
her jewels sold in secret to pay their bills;
and lament only for happiness lost.

Yet even without the blackmail and bullying
of the father's intervention, Violetta's surrender
speaks of a passion foreign to our age, when
people are supposed to move off for their own good;
and friends to chivvy them out of such obsessions.
Why should she spend herself to the last cough of blood?

The tears give another answer. Looking around,
in the ENO audience, I see women weeping
on every side, as if such commitment arouses
a profound longing; we may refuse to be sacrificed,
but respond to the fiction, are betrayed
in the music, and not only in opera houses.

Casualty

A green computer called George is reading
my vital signs through a peg on an index finger.
I try to understand the bleeps, while the Ibo nurse
chuckles and gives his rusty stand a kick:
'This one, he's unreliable old thing.'

Four a.m. She leaves, and then it's lonely.
Even George has gone now, though eight leads
are still attached to my chest and legs. I'm
knackered, but I can't sleep on the trolley
and there's nothing here to look at but a shelf

of cardboard piss pots and an oxygen mask,
the bin for contaminated spikes, and a
red button to be pushed in asthmatic spasm.
Impatient for daylight, tossing in my cot,
thoughts rattle in my head: I want

my ordinary life back. What
a mistake to let an ambulance
carry me off to this wretched ward.
There may be nothing much wrong.
That sudden hope rises in me like birdsong.

Freedom

When you are out, I wander round the flat,
eat fruit, read newspapers and do
surprisingly less work. No doubt of that.

So what am I missing? Are you right to claim
a blown up effigy, sitting in a chair
would be the same?

Not quite. The poem's space may
seem to offer its own escape, but I still need
the goad of words that find their mark.

When I look down through glass
to see you getting out of a black cab,
frazzled, hair wild, and raincoat open,

fumbling for change, and know that
you are neither lost nor hurt – it's brief,
but what I feel is passionate relief.

Respite

Rain in the beech trees at 4 a.m.:
I ran away from your voice to
sit in an upright chair. Useless
in your despair, I had no
strength to scoop you
out of your long story,
let alone think of rescue.

Somewhere, the elfin child
of your tinted sepia photo
was still bravely smiling,
with a nail of ice in his heart.
And how can we be reconciled
to that, or hope to unfreeze
what has been so long frozen?

Then you struggled, on sticks,
to my side. You kissed my fingers,
and face, begging me back into bed,
calling me good and kind.
And generous words of love
flowed on all night long, as if
they healed your flashing mind.

Prayer for my Son

Most things I worry over never happen,
but this, disguised as an embarrassment,
turned risky in a day. Two years ago,
from the furthest edge of a blue sky,
an illness snatched his livelihood away.

Justice, Lord? How is this just? I
muttered, as if every generation must
learn the lesson again: there is
no special privilege protecting us.
He lay across his futon, white and thin

– the QEH sold out, his dep chosen –
in double torment. No one could comfort him.
I would have kissed the feet
of any holy man – as the Shunamite
woman did – to have the Lord relent.

But what since the miracle of his recovery?
Petty angers, like a girlish sulk. Forgive
me such ingratitude. Let him only live
with grace, unthreatened, on the sound of his flute
– and I'll stop clamouring for sweeter fruit.

Wasp

The Singleton is fiercer than the rest.
Who would have guessed?
A sleepy wriggle will provoke the thing.

My leg is swollen red with histamine.
Doctors say from now on I must live
in fear of another sting.

Immortal wasp, only last October
I put your crippled body out the window
and here you are again, buzzing with Spring.

City Lights

for Fisher at seventy

Roy, I'm fussed by festschrifts.
Even when I promise
a piece, I either miss
the deadlines, or the lines
themselves fall dead.

I learnt from you that poems
can be lit by zinc, and smell
of currants or petrol; I
walked the wet streets
of your city memories,

hearing that childhood sneer
of the Midlands in my ear:
'You *what*? You must be joking.'
In Cambridge, at the Erard,
yours was a nimble answer.

Dud keys sounded for your fingers.
Let me salute you then, as jazz man,
stand up comic, fellow poet, and
for many years my bookshop companion –
filed under F – as another outsider.

Exile

i.m. Andrew Kelus

It was what you wanted, your friend told me.
Your creditors had been anticipated.

They will not evict you now from your apartment
hanging over the river in Basel. Yet

it was your extravagance I loved, the absurd
gesture of taking us, with three children

for snails in garlic butter at the Rhinekeller.
It was a generosity you couldn't afford

even then, even before young men
and beautiful possessions had consumed

whatever you earned. I remember
once you took an army knife away

from a mugger working the New York subway,
because you had seen he was afraid.

I know that other people often paid
for your recklessness, but in defence,

you shared with them your own talent for
revelling in joy more than common sense.

Encounter

Afloat in October, my birthday month
in Baltic sunshine, my mouth satisfied
with coarse russet apples, their flesh
yellow rather than white, I lay down

to sleep where there was starlight
and the sound of water and dreamed
of the desert. There were leaf shadows
and watery light, and an unknown

presence in a pile of stones.
Whether the man who wrestled
with me all night long was good
or evil, he blessed me at first light.

In Praise of Flair

That whole wet summer, I listened to Louis Armstrong.
Imagined him arriving in New York after Funky Butt
dance halls, wearing hick clothes: those
high top shoes with hooks, and long
underwear down to his socks.

Thought of him shy in a slick, new band, locked
for two weeks reading the part he was set,
until the night when Bailey on clarinet
took over an old song. Then Louis' horn
rose in harsh, elated notes,

of phrases he'd invented on riverboats
and ratty blues tonks, using all the sinews
of his face and muscle of his tongue.
And what delights me now,
is when he grinned to thank

the crowd that stood to clap, and saw
slyly from the corner of his eye
all the stingy players in the band
were sitting motionless, their tribute
only an astonished sigh.

Options

Illicit one-time love, your face
was narrow as mine, Italian as
De Niro. You were fortunate
to escape marriage to me, yet
sometimes, I confess, you visit
my salacious dreams. I wear black
lycra above the knee, and meet
your eyes as if you were an eager
punter on Great Windmill Street

It's years since I gave back your rose cut
diamond ring – which didn't show much wit –
so why would I think of calling you this evening
half way across the world? I have
your number, but see no point using it.
It's far too late for an alternative life.
You would have hated being strapped for cash.
And who can tell how long we would have
burned together, before turning to ash?

Snowdonia

Black on white, a roadside, a shock
of mountain rock: I am looking in
through a photo found in an Indian tin,
to a piece of my lost history.
There on my father's knee,
my hair cut like Clara Bow,
I can't have been more than three.

Do I remember, or is it a dream
that the group of relations, resting
on stones, are exhausted to mutiny,
while my father continues to urge us upward?
My eyes look shyly under my fringe
at whatever he wants me to see.

For a moment I imagine his voice.
'The air, taste the air.' And my throat
tightens, searching the square
of a black and white photo,
a band of ghosts, and a
mountain's majestic glare.

Boatsong

Looking at figures of flicked ink
trudging up hills of snow, their plan
panning for gold in the Klondike:
that is *one* mistake, I think
I was unlikely to make.

People usually choose the shape
of the dangers they undertake:
anchor men, traders in futures
dealers in crack cocaine
all select the style of their fear.

So what am I doing here?
On dark waters near Torquay
once as a child, I let myself drift
on a lilo out to sea,
and was lucky to survive.

Now in my study I sail along
trawling for words to feel alive.
And that is my rush of adrenalin
with muggy London air in the lungs,
and oil of wintergreen on my skin.

Galway

At the Breton restaurant in Galway
the claws of huge brown lobsters caught
in the Atlantic wave are still moving.
Do we lie to ourselves about everything?
They will boil slowly into restaurant red.

Two swans extend their necks in lines of muscle.
They live on fish here, not tourist bread.
And they, at least, are wild as poetry;
the shuffle of book-signings is nothing to them.
Let us eat and drink well away from the jostle.

We may be remembered, perhaps by strangers,
but none of us will need to burn our lines.
These days we say what we like, even
in Russia, as if no one is truly listening.
Here in the South, Ireland is eerily booming.

Bells

Big Ben sounds cold tonight.
Each strike an ache of ice.
My neck feels every gong
as a chill. The traffic halts
and the radio news has
a wartime, childhood voice.

Bong. An honourable war,
and simple politics. *Bong.*
We sit in the car and absorb
the rhetoric of peace.
And I remember VE day,
jiving with friendly Yanks,

or sitting in the cinema
applauding Russian tanks.
Bong. Dead bodies fill
our telly screen. Who will
suggest a remedy? For God
was not the Commandmant

who set up Uncle Jo's Gulag
or sent Emma Lazarus' children off
to napalm gooks across Vietnam.
We did it. *Bong.* The human ape,
inheritor of planet earth, and
from our power there's no escape.

Gypsies

'Those black eyed children begging in Bucharest
are all pickpockets,' smiled our exquisite hostess,
who had set a table for us with fresh cucumber,
and sliced tomatoes. 'From the country,' she explained
the delicacy, rare in present-day Rumania.

Crossing the gaunt and treeless plain near Craiova,
we noticed houses painted like caravans,
With curving roofs and colours quaintly Asian.
Our driver said they were owned by rich Gypsies,
'They go to East Germany and steal Mercedes.'

'You know, Gypsies are hated over there,'
I mused to my London newsagent, looking at
a headline about stowaways caught in Dover.
But he, with his sad Pakistani eyes, replied,
'Why are they so hated? They must be bad.'

Revolutions

If you've seen Pontecorvo's *Battle of Algiers*,
you'll remember: the bombs ticking in French cafés
while babies lick ice-cream, the FLN bodies hanging
their heads dunked in urinals, everything
black and white like documentary footage.
The film took the *Lion D'Or* in '66.

All through the fifties, we puzzled at French officers
using torture, wasn't Colonel Mathieu a member
of the old Resistance? Yet they behaved like Nazis.
Our children would be amazed at our innocence,
but they were babies then, or unborn, and nowadays
television has educated everyone in the commonplace

ubiquity of cruelty, the logic of it. It's become
a disgusting part of what we see as human.
So the Algerian Revolution was finally won
but men gave their lives to displace one tyranny
and had it replaced by another. It may be those
most willing to die make their point, but where's the victory?

Gluttony

A ballad after the manner of Bert Brecht

Now people say we ought to curb our appetite –
Unhealthy eating has to be abhorred;
And yet we savour each illicit, risky bite
Of dangerous delights we can't afford.
For only pride dictates we should be thin
Whatever choice we make will be a sin.

Our bodies may be damaged eating too much fat
So, to be safe, what we prefer to choose
Will not occlude this or be furring that.
There's precious little else that we refuse.
Mushrooms and rocket salad, with a tin
Of caviar is quite a modest sin.

To Marks and Spencers' finest new emporium
We travel through the winter's dark to buy
Red salmon eggs, or breast of leanest duck in plum,
Whatever luxuries they can supply.
Addiction to these pleasures is a sin
Less dodgy than a shot of heroin.

At rich relations' tables we sometimes enjoy
Foie gras of goose with port and caramel
Or sushi salmon delicately spiced with soy,
Thick white asparagus that's buttered well.
These are the perks reluctant Duty wins.
Why should we need to speak of them as sins?

We relish halibut in cream and cognac –
Honey glazed sea bass with a crisp white wine.
Although the sweets are more than we can knock back –
Only a sour curmudgeon would decline.
In my politeness, I'm a heroine.
Who can describe such courtesy as sin?

Our glittering consumer world depends on it,
Since where there's profit, nothing is malign;
Moreover, all the food we eat will turn to shit,
A useful link in Nature's Grand Design.
If you pretend that Gluttony's a sin
Forgive me, but I can't repress a grin …

Unless there sits outside the supermarket door
Some homeless wreck who shivers in his hunger
I give him my small change, and sometimes more –
My conscience, I suppose, that old scaremonger.
Is he a loser, so the rest can win,
Or is that reassuring thought a sin?

Splitting

To slash, split open or break.
To sever or smash or crack.
The word for leaving a partner amounts
to violent dismemberment,
yet others perform the act.

So is it courage she lacks?
Is she held by compassion – or fear?
Does she want to believe if
she gambles on going, he'll
wait for her to come back?

Powerbook. Disks. All packed.
His shrink told her years ago:
'He can give you nothing. Try
to detach yourself if you can.' So why
does she go on loving the man?

Poet

The last days of October were dark and wet.
In our London street, a brown rain flooded
the gutters with fallen leaves, and at night
a wind shook the branches of the trees
like a child's rattle. In the countryside,
rivers poured into village houses.

The weather got into our dreams in the figure
of Ted Hughes. One of us, asleep in a chair,
spent the night wandering round his
Devon house, staring through
picture windows in the storm, unable
to find a way outside.

In my mind, he was standing in our old
Cambridge kitchen, his face like mountain stone,
his presence solemn and kind. He bestowed
a gift of abalone shells, without ceremony.
This morning, on the telephone,
his sister called to tell us he had died.

It was almost as if his spirit
in its passing, had casually touched
a synapse. He never needed to stir
to draw attention in a room, the magnet
of his being pulled everyone to him;
now his after-image flashed within us.

We travelled through fields of mud
towards North Tawton Church and funeral,
seeing wet dogs and hovering birds
as he had: all creatures of a brutal
planet, to be observed with love, knowing
their cruelties include the human animal.

Jeopardy

All year I've watched the velvet glow
of your happiness, seen you flow
towards him, while he bathes in your spirit;
a glittering exchange of tongue and wit.
I've known what you wanted most was
the risk of giving without calculation.

Now he consumes your pleasure along
with grapes, tree fungus, red nectar,
and since he is no ordinary sailor,
takes the island for his own, as he
receives your enchanted songs.
Calypso, Calypso,

What he gives in return is splendour:
partly his own, and partly the mirror
in which you perceive your own beauty:
the sum of everything he ever loved.
Relishing the energy of his self-concern,
you have already forgiven his onward journey.

Uncollected Poems

September Song

for Danny and Valentina

A light sleeper in his Venetian bed,
    Joseph Brodsky is dreaming this ceremony.
The streets of London still run through his head
    — I write in rhyme, feeling his eye upon me —
as he turns over his old Summer days
    in Hampstead, remembering Flask Walk,
and Brendel. His immortal musing plays
    over young writers, listening to him talk
on their scuffed armchairs. Since he took a hand
    in bringing these two friends of his together
through poetry, today he's on the Strand:
    to watch a Jew always in love with Russia
marry his pepper-vodka Valentina.

The maple has begun its Autumn burn
    but trees are leafy still in mid-September
and relish sunlight as the seasons turn.
    Forget the Kurt Weill melody, remember:
a special passion marks a late marriage:
    the grand abandoning of old sorrows
to welcome hope. This couple has-the courage,
    to ask a blessing on their shared tomorrows.
Let us imagine Brodsky raising a toast
    'to say the least' on this lucky occasion.
His spirit will not be the only ghost
    hovering overhead in conversation.
For many who have been this couple's mentors
    gather above us to approve the scene
as two bold spirits on whom this day centres
    prepare to live in London's Golders Green.
Let them have champagne, caviare and roses,
    and feel most happy as the party closes.

Hotel Maimonides

1

Bewildered in the glories of abundance,
imagine how our dead poets and scholars
would thread the cool streets of this Jewish quarter
and ask where is the scabrous past, the birdcages
the women in black clothes carrying herbs,
to Christian fires. After five centuries

the names on this square are of refugees
who took their skills away to Syria,
their languages, their medicine, their patience
and now by the great Mosque of Cordova
where jewellers sell rings of garnets in silver
they wander invisibly among tourists

puzzled to learn a Hebrew ancestor
is now more prized than limpieza de sangre.
In Spain, they love our ghosts. And we
who relish heaped fruits, a sleep post lunch
and sweet melocoton in this hotel
so grandly named after Maimonides[1]

remain perplexed for all his guidance.
What will become of you now, my people
who returned from the Yemen on a white bird
that dropped out of the sky, or from their
scattering across North Africa and Uzbekistan
to claim a homeland? The history is not encouraging.

---

1 Moses Maimonides was a Jewish philosopher, physician and scholar. His most
famous work is *Guide to the Perplexed*.

2

At home in Belsize Park as I wake to
the lark and the wren at 4 am and marvel
at the poise of birch trees after winter rain,
while the fresh leaves shiver in the subtle
grey light. I am disturbed
by another question:

What has the fanatic Middle East
to do with me? My grandparents
are buried in British earth, my children
are married out, my newspapers
concerned for the oppressed in camps, my synagogue
in dialogue with Said and Ashrawi.

Why are my dreams disturbed
by crossing borders, hiding, stories
of angry peasants and sly priests
when I look over a quiet garden
lit with pale sunshine? It is because
I have lived in a rare island of peace

where it is far too easy to be liberal
with desperate terrain for the dispossessed.
Over there, my secular friends battle
stubbornly to defend a coastal strip,
with negotiations sadly no longer the issue,
uncertain the world accords them the right to exist.

Translations

MARINA TSVETAYEVA*

Verses

written so long ago, I didn't even
    know I was a poet,
my words fell like spray from a fountain
    or flashes from a rocket,

like brats, they burst into sanctuaries
    asleep and filled with incense,
to speak of youth and mortality.
    And now my unread pages

lie scattered in dusty bookshops
    where nobody even lifts them
to examine. And yet, like expensive wines,
    your time will come, my lines.

May 1913

Anna

Your narrow, foreign shape
    is bent over written papers,
and a Turkish shawl is dropped
    around you like a cloak.

You make a single line, which
    is broken and black at once.
You are equally cold – in erotic
    gaiety – or unhappiness.

* A list of collaborators can be found on p. 305.

All your life is a fever to be
    flawless, and yet this young
demon, who on earth is she
    with her cloudy, dark face?

Everyone else is worldly,
    while you remain playful,
your harmless lines of poetry
    are toys – aimed at the heart.

So in a sleepy, morning hour –
    at five a.m. – I discover
I've fallen in love with you,
    Anna Akhmatova

                                    1915

I know the truth

I know the truth – give up all other truths!
No need for people anywhere on earth to struggle.
Look – it is evening, look, it is nearly night:
what do you speak of, poets, lovers, generals?

The wind is level now, the earth is wet with dew,
the storm of stars in the sky will turn to quiet.
And soon all of us will sleep under the earth, we
who never let each other sleep above it.

                                    1915

What is this gypsy passion for separation

What is this gypsy passion for separation, this
    readiness to rush off – when we've just met?
My head rests in my hands as I
    realise, looking into the night

that no one turning over our letters has
    yet understood how completely and
how deeply faithless we are, which is
    to say: how true we are to ourselves.

1915

We shall not escape Hell

We shall not escape Hell, my passionate
sisters, we shall drink black resins –
we who sang our praises to the Lord
with every one of our sinews, even the finest,

we did not lean over cradles or
spinning wheels at night, and now we are
carried off by an unsteady boat
under the skirts of a sleeveless cloak,

we dressed every morning in
fine Chinese silk, and we would
sing our paradisal songs at
the fire of the robbers' camp,

slovenly needlewomen, (all
our sewing came apart), dancers,
players upon pipes: we have been
the queens of the whole world!

first scarcely covered by rags,
then with constellations in our hair, in
gaol and at feasts we have
bartered away heaven,

in starry nights, in the apple
orchards of Paradise.
– Gentle girls, my beloved sisters,
we shall certainly find ourselves in Hell!

1915

Some ancestor of mine

Some ancestor of mine was a violinist
    and a thief into the bargain.
Does this explain my vagrant disposition
    and hair that smells of the wind?

Dark, curly-haired, hooknosed, he is
    the one who steals apricots
from the cart, using my hand. Yes,
    he is responsible for my fate.

Admiring the ploughman at his labour,
    he used to twirl a dog rose
in his lips. He was always unreliable
    as a friend, but a tender lover.

Fond of his pipe, the moon, beads, and all
    the young women in the neighbourhood ...
I think he may have also been a coward,
    my yellow-eyed ancestor.

His soul was sold for a farthing,
    so he did not walk at midnight
in the cemetery. He may have worn
    a knife tucked in his boot.

Perhaps he pounced round corners
like a sinuous cat.
I wonder suddenly: did
he even play the violin?

I know nothing mattered to him
any more than last year's snow.
That's what he was like, my ancestor.
And that's the kind of poet I am.

1915

I'm glad your sickness

I'm glad your sickness is not caused by me.
Mine is not caused by you. I'm glad to know
the heavy earth will never flow away
from us, beneath our feet, and so
we can relax together, and not watch
our words. When our sleeves touch
we shall not drown in waves of rising blush.

I'm glad to see you calmly now embrace
another girl in front of me, without
any wish to cause me pain, as you
don't burn if I kiss someone else.
I know you never use my tender name,
my tender spirit, day or night. And
no one in the silence of a church
will sing their Hallelujahs over us.

Thank you for loving me like this,
for you feel love, although you do not know it.
Thank you for the nights I've spent in quiet.
Thank you for the walks under the moon
you've spared me and those sunset meetings unshared.
Thank you. The sun will never bless our heads.
Take my sad thanks for this: you do not cause
my sickness. And I don't cause yours.

1915

We are keeping an eye on the girls

We are keeping an eye on the girls, so that the *kvass*
doesn't go sour in the jug, or the pancakes cold,
counting over the rings, and pouring Anis
into the long bottles with their narrow throats,

straightening tow thread for the peasant woman:
filling the house with the fresh smoke of
incense   and we are sailing over Cathedral square
arm in arm with our godfather, silks thundering.

The wet nurse has a screeching cockerel
in her apron – her clothes are like the night.
She announces in an ancient whisper that
a dead young man   lies in the chapel.

And an incense cloud wraps the corners
under its own saddened chasuble.
The apple trees are white, like angels – and
the pigeons on them – grey – like incense itself.

And the pilgrim woman sipping *kvass* from the ladle
on the edge of the couch, is telling
to the very end a tale about Razin
and his most beautiful Persian girl.

1916

No one has taken anything away

No one has taken anything away –
      there is even a sweetness for me in being apart.
I kiss you now across the many
      hundreds of miles that separate us.

I know: our gifts are unequal, which is
    why my voice is – quiet, for the first time.
What can my untutored verse
    matter to you, a young Derzhavin?

For your terrible flight I give you blessing.
    Fly, then, young eagle! You
have stared into the sun without blinking.
    Can my young gaze be too heavy for you?

No one has ever stared more
    tenderly or more fixedly after you ...
I kiss you – across hundreds of
    separating years.

1916

You throw back your head

You throw back your head, because
you are proud. And a braggart.
This February has
brought me a gay companion!

Clattering with gold pieces, and
slowly puffing out smoke, we
walk like solemn foreigners
throughout my native city.

And whose attentive hands have
touched your eyelashes, beautiful boy, and
when or how many times your
lips have been kissed

I do not ask. That dream my thirsty
spirit has conquered. Now
I can honour in you the
divine boy, ten years old!

Let us wait by the river that
rinses the coloured beads of street-lights:
I shall take you as far as the square
that has witnessed adolescent Tsars.

Whistle out your boyish
pain, your heart squeezed in your hand.
My indifferent and crazy creature –
now set free – goodbye!

1916

Where does this tenderness come from?

Where does this tenderness come from?
These are not the – first curls I
have stroked slowly – and lips I
have known are – darker than yours

as stars rise often and go out again
(where does this tenderness come from?)
so many eyes have risen and died out
        in front of these eyes of mine.

and yet no such song have
I heard in the darkness of night before,
(where does this tenderness come from?):
        here, on the ribs of the singer.

Where does this tenderness come from?
And what shall I do with it, young
sly singer, just passing by?
Your lashes are – longer than anyone's.

1916

Bent with worry

Bent with worry, God
    paused, to smile.
And look, there were many
holy angels with bodies of

the radiance he had
    given them,
some with enormous wings and
others without any,

which is why I weep
    so much
because even more than God
himself I love his fair angels.

1916

Today or tomorrow the snow will melt

Today or tomorrow the snow will melt.
You lie alone beneath an enormous fur.
Shall I pity you? Your lips
have gone dry for ever.

Your drinking is difficult, your step heavy.
Every passer-by hurries away from you.
Was it with fingers like yours that Rogozhin
clutched the garden knife?

And the eyes, the eyes in your face!
Two circles of charcoal, year-old circles!
Surely when you were still young your girl
lured you into a joyless house.

Far away – in the night – over asphalt – a cane.
Doors – swing open into – night – under beating wind.
Come in! Appear! Undesired guest! Into
my chamber which is – most bright!

1916

Verses about Moscow

1

There are clouds – about us
and domes – about us:
over the whole of Moscow
so many hands are needed!
I lift you up like a
sapling, my best burden: for
to me you are   weightless.

In this city of wonder
this peaceful city
I shall be joyful, even
when I am dead. You
shall reign, or grieve
or perhaps receive my crown:
for you are my first born!

When you fast – in Lent
do not blacken your brows
and honour the churches – these
forty times forty – go
about on foot – stride youthfully
over the whole seven of
these untrammelled hills.

Your turn will come.
You will give Moscow
with tender bitterness
to your daughter also.

As for me – unbroken sleep
and the sound of bells
in the surly dawn of
the Vagankovo cemetery.

2

Strange and beautiful brother – take this
city no hands built – out of my hands!

Church by church – all the forty times forty, and
the small pigeons also that rise over them.

Take the Spassky gate, with its flowers, where
the orthodox remove their caps, and

the chapel of stars, that refuge from evil,
where the floor is polished by kisses.

Take from me the incomparable circle
of five cathedrals, ancient, holy friend!

I shall lead you as a guest from another
country to the Chapel of the Inadvertent Joy

where pure gold domes will begin to shine
for you, and sleepless bells will start thundering.

There the Mother of God will drop her
cloak upon you from the crimson clouds

and you will rise up filled with wonderful powers.
Then, you will not repent that you have loved me!

5

Over the city that great Peter rejected
rolls out the thunder of the bells.

A thundering surf has overturned upon
this woman you have now rejected.

I offer homage to Peter and you also,
yet above you both the bells remain

and while they thunder from that blueness, the
primacy of Moscow cannot be questioned

for all the forty times forty churches
laugh above the arrogance of Tsars.

7

There are seven hills – like seven bells,
seven bells, seven bell-towers. Every
one of the forty times forty churches, and the
seven hills of bells have been numbered.

On a day of bells I was born, it was
the golden day of John the Divine.
The house was gingerbread surrounded by
wattle-fence, and small churches with gold heads.

And I loved it, I loved the first ringing,
the nuns flowing towards Mass, and
the wailing in the stone, the heat of sleeping –
the sense of a soothsayer in the neighbouring house.

Come with me, people of Moscow, all of you,
imbecile, thieving, flagellant mob!
And priest: stop my mouth up firmly
with Moscow – which is a land of bells!

8

Moscow, what a vast
hostelry is your house!
Everyone in Russia is – homeless,
we shall all make our way towards you.

With shameful brands on our backs and
knives – stuck in the tops of our boots,
for you call us in to you
however far away we are,

because for the brand of the criminal
and for every known sickness
we have our healer here,
the Child Panteleimon.

Behind a small door where
people pour in their crowds
lies the Iversky heart –
red-gold and radiant

and a Hallelujah floods
over the burnished fields.
Moscow soil, I bend to
kiss your breast.

1916

From *Insomnia*

2

As I love to
   kiss hands, and
to name everything, I
   love to open
doors!
   Wide – into the night!

Pressing my head
   as I listen to some
heavy step grow softer
   or the wind shaking
the sleepy and sleepless
   woods.

Ah, night
    small rivers of water rise
and bend towards – sleep.
    (I am nearly sleeping.)
Somewhere in the night a
    human being is drowning.

3

In my enormous city it is – night,
as from my sleeping house I go – out,
and people think perhaps I'm a daughter or wife
but in my mind is one thought only: night.

The July wind now sweeps a way for – me.
From somewhere, some window, music though – faint.
The wind can blow until the dawn – today,
in through the fine walls of the breast rib-cage.

Black poplars, windows, filled with – light.
Music from high buildings, in my hand a flower.
Look at my steps – following – nobody.
Look at my shadow, nothing's here of me.

The lights – are like threads of golden beads
in my mouth is the taste of the night – leaf.
Liberate me from the bonds of – day,
my friends, understand: I'm nothing but your dream.

5

Now as a guest from heaven, I
    visit your country:
I have seen the vigil of the forests
    and sleep in the fields.

Somewhere in the night horseshoes
    have torn up the grass, and
there are cows breathing heavily in
    a sleepy cowshed.

Now let me tell you sadly and
    with tenderness of the
goose-watchman awake, and
    the sleeping geese,

of hands immersed in dog's wool,
    grey hair – a grey dog –
and how towards six
    the dawn is beginning.

6

Tonight – I am alone in the night,
    a homeless and sleepless nun!
Tonight I hold all the keys to this
    the only capital city

and lack of sleep guides me on my path.
    You are so lovely, my dusky Kremlin!
Tonight I put my lips to the breast
    of the whole round and warring earth.

Now I feel hair – like fur – standing on end
    the stifling wind blows straight into my soul.
Tonight I feel compassion for everyone,
    those who are pitied, along with those who are kissed.

7

In the pine-tree, tenderly tenderly,
    finely finely: something hissed.
It is a child with black
    eyes that I see in my sleep.

From the fair pine-trees hot
    resin drips, and in this
splendid night there are
    saw-teeth going over my heart.

Black as – the centre of an eye, the centre, a blackness
that sucks at light. I love your vigilance

Night, first mother of songs, give me the voice to sing of you
in those fingers lies the bridle of the four winds.

Crying out, offering words of homage to you, I am
only a shell where the ocean is still sounding.

But I have looked too long into human eyes.
Reduce me now to ashes – Night, like a black sun.

9

Who sleeps at night? No one is sleeping.
   In the cradle a child is screaming.
An old man sits over his death, and anyone
   young enough talks to his love, breathes
into her lips, looks into her eyes.

Once asleep – who knows if we'll wake again?
We have time, we have time, we have time to sleep!

From house to house the sharp-eyed
   watchman goes with his pink lantern
and over the pillow scatters the rattle
   of his loud clapper, rumbling.

Don't sleep! Be firm! Listen, the alternative
is – everlasting sleep. Your – everlasting house!

10

Here's another window
with more sleepless people!
Perhaps – drinking wine or
perhaps only sitting,
or maybe two lovers are
unable to part hands.
Every house has
a window like this.

A window at night: cries
of meeting or leaving.
Perhaps – there are many lights,
perhaps – only three candles.
But there is no peace in
my mind anywhere, for
in my house also, these
things are beginning:

Pray for the wakeful house,
friend, and the lit window.

1916

Poems for Akhmatova

1

Muse of lament, you are the most beautiful of
    all muses, a crazy emanation of white night:
and you have sent a black snow storm over all Russia.
    We are pierced with the arrows of your cries

so that we shy like horses at the muffled
    many times uttered pledge – Ah! – Anna
Akhmatova – the name is a vast sigh
    and it falls into depths without name

and we wear crowns only through stamping
　　the same earth as you, with the same sky over us.
Whoever shares the pain of your deathly power will
　　lie down immortal – upon his death bed.

In my melodious town the domes are burning
　　and the blind wanderer praises our shining Lord.
I give you my town of many bells,
　　Akhmatova, and with the gift: my heart.

2

I stand　　head in my hands　　thinking how
　　unimportant are the traps we set for one another
I hold my head in my hands　　as I sing
　　in this late hour, in the late dawn.

Ah how violent is this wave which has
　　lifted me up on to its crest: I sing
of one　　　that is unique among us
　　as the moon is　　alone in the sky,

that has flown into my heart like a raven.
　　has speared into the clouds
hook-nosed, with deathly anger: even
　　your favour is　　dangerous,

for you have spread out your night
　　over the pure gold of my Kremlin itself
and have tightened my throat with the pleasure
　　of singing　　as if with a strap.

Yes, I am happy, the dawn never
　　burnt with more purity, I am
happy to give everything to you
　　and to go away　　like a beggar,

for I was the first to give you –
　　whose voice　　deep darkness!　　has
constricted the movement of my breathing –
　　the name of the Tsarskoselsky Muse.

I am a convict. You won't fall behind.
You are my guard. Our fate is therefore one.
And in that emptiness that we both share
the same command to ride away is given.

And now my demeanour is calm.
And now   my eyes are without guile.
Won't you set me free, my guard, and
let me walk now, towards that pine-tree?

4

You block out everything, even the sun
    at its highest, hold all the stars in your hand!
If only through – some wide open door, I
    could blow like the wind to where you are,

and starting to stammer, suddenly blushing,
    could lower my eyes before you
and fall quiet, in tears, as
    a child sobs to receive forgiveness.

1916

Poems for Blok

1

Your name is a – bird in my hand
a piece of – ice on the tongue
one single movement of the lips.
Your name is: five signs,
a ball caught in flight, a
silver bell in the mouth

a stone, cast in a quiet pool
makes the splash of your name, and
the sound is in the clatter of
night hooves, loud as a thunderclap
or it speaks straight into my forehead,
shrill as the click of a cocked gun.

Your name – how impossible, it
is a kiss in the eyes on
motionless eyelashes, chill and sweet.
Your name is a kiss of snow
a gulp of icy spring water, blue
as a dove. About your name is: sleep.

1916

2

Tender – spectre
blameless as a knight, who
has called you into
my adolescent life?

In blue dark, grey
and priestly, you
stand here, dressed in snow.

And it's not the wind
that drives me through the town now.
No, this is the third
night I felt the old enemy.

With light blue eyes his
magic has bound
me, that snowy singer:

swan of snow, under
my feet he spreads his feathers.
Hovering feathers,
slowly they dip in the snow.

Thus upon feathers
I go, towards the door
behind which is: death.

He sings to me
behind the blue windows.
He sings to me
as jewelled bells.

Long is the shout from
his swan's beak as
he calls.

Dear spectre of
mist I know this is dreaming,
so one favour now, do
for me, amen: of dispersing.
Amen, amen.

1916

3

You are going – west of the sun now.
You will see there – evening light.
You are going – west of the sun and
snow will cover up your tracks.

Past my windows – passionless
you are going in quiet snow.
Saint of God, beautiful, you
are the quiet light of my soul

but I do not long for your spirit.
Your way is indestructible.
And your hand is pale from holy
kisses, no nail of mine.

By your name I shall not call you.
My hands shall not stretch after you
to your holy waxen face I shall
only bow – from afar

standing under the slow falling snow, I shall
fall to my knees – in the snow.
In your holy name I shall only
kiss that evening snow

where, with majestic pace you
go by in tomb-like quiet,
the light of quiet – holy glory
of it: Keeper of my soul.

1916

5

At home in Moscow – where the domes are burning,
at home in Moscow – in the sound of bells,
where I live the tombs – in their rows are standing
and in them Tsaritsas – are asleep and Tsars.

And you don't know how – at dawn the Kremlin is
the easiest place to – breathe in the whole wide earth
and you don't know when – dawn reaches the Kremlin
I pray to you until – the next day comes

and I go with you – by your river Neva
even while beside – the Moscow river
I am standing here – with my head lowered
and the line of street lights – sticks fast together.

With my insomnia – I love you wholly.
With my insomnia – I listen for you,
just at the hour throughout – the Kremlin, men
who ring the bells – begin to waken.

Still my river – and your river
still my hand – and your hand
will never join, or not until
one dawn catches up another dawning.

1916

8

And the gadflies gather about indifferent cart-horses,
the red calico of Kaluga puffs out in the wind,
it is a time of whistling quails and huge skies,
bells waving over waves of corn, and more
talk about Germans than anyone can bear.
Now yellow, yellow, beyond the blue trees is a
cross, and a sweet fever, a radiance over
everything: your name   sounding like *angel.*

1916

9

A weak shaft of light through the blackness of hell is
his voice under the rumble of exploding shells

in that thunder like a seraph he is announcing
in a toneless voice, from somewhere else, some

ancient misty morning he inhabits, how he
loved us, who are blind and nameless   who

share the blue cloak of   sinful treachery
and more tenderly than anyone loved the woman who

sank so daringly into the night   of evil,
and of his love for you, Russia, which he cannot end.

And he draws an absent-minded finger along
his temple   all the time he tells us of

the days that wait for us, how God will deceive us.
We shall call for the sun and it will not rise.

He spoke like a solitary prisoner
(or perhaps a child speaking to himself)

so that over the whole square the sacred
heart of Alexander Blok appeared to us.

1920

6

Thinking him   human   they
decided to kill him, and
now he's dead. For ever.
– Weep. For the dead angel.

At the day's setting, he
sang the evening beauty.
Three waxen lights now
shudder superstitiously

and lines of light, hot
strings across the snow come from him.
Three waxen candles.
To the sun. The light-bearer.

O now look how
dark his eyelids are fallen,
O now look how
his wings are broken.

The black reciter reads.
The people idly stamp.
Dead lies the singer, and
celebrates resurrection.

1916

10

Look there he is, weary from foreign parts,
a leader without body-guard

there – he is drinking a mountain stream from his hands
a prince without native land.

He has everything in his holy princedom there
Army, bread and mother.

Lovely is your inheritance.
Govern, friend without friends.

1921

A kiss on the head

A kiss on the head – wipes away misery.
I kiss your head.

A kiss on the eyes – takes away sleeplessness.
I kiss your eyes.

A kiss on the lips – quenches the deepest thirst.
I kiss your lips.

A kiss on the head – wipes away memory.
I kiss your head.

1917

From *Swans' Encampment*

Little mushroom, white Bolitus,
               my own favourite
The field sways, a chant of Rus'
               rises over it.
Help me, I'm unsteady on my feet.
This blood-red is making my eyes foggy.

On either side, mouths lie
open and bleeding, and from
each wound rises a cry:
– Mother!

One word is all I hear, as
I stand dazed. From someone
else's womb   into my own:
– Mother!

They all lie in a row,
no line between them,
I recognise that each one was a soldier.
But which is mine? Which one is another's?

This man was White   now he's become Red.
Blood has reddened him.
This one was Red   now he's become White.
Death has whitened him.

– What are you? White? – Can't understand!
                    – Lean on your arm!
Have you been with the Reds?
                    – Ry   -azan.

And so from right and left
Behind   ahead
together, White and Red, one cry of
– Mother!

Without choice. Without anger.
One long moan. Stubbornly.
A cry that reaches up to heaven,
– Mother!

                                        1917–21

Yesterday he still looked in my eyes

Yesterday he still looked in my eyes, yet
      today   his looks are bent aside.   Yesterday
he sat here until the birds began, but
today   all those larks are   ravens.

Stupid creature! And you are wise, you
      live while I am stunned.
Now for the lament of women in all times:
      – My love, what was it I did to you?

And tears are   water, blood is   water,
      a woman always washes in blood and tears.
Love is a step-mother, and no mother:
      then expect no justice or mercy from her.

Ships carry away the ones we love.
  Along the white road they are taken away.
And one cry stretches across the earth:
  — My love, what was it I did to you?

Yesterday he lay at my feet. He even
  compared me with the Chinese empire! Then
suddenly he let his hands fall open, and
  my life fell out like   a rusty kopeck.

A child-murderer, before some court
  I stand   loathsome and timid I am.
And yet even in Hell I shall demand:
  — My love, what was it I did to you?

I ask this chair, I ask the bed: Why?
  Why do I suffer and live in penury?
His kisses stopped. He wanted to break you.
  To kiss another girl is their reply.

He taught me to live in fire, he threw me there,
  and then abandoned me on steppes of ice.
My love, I know what you have done to me.
  — My love, what was it I did to you?

I know everything, don't argue with me!
  I can see now, I'm a lover no longer.
And now I know wherever love holds power
  Death approaches soon   like a gardener.

It is almost like shaking a tree, in time
  some ripe apple comes falling down. So
for everything, for everything   forgive me,
  — my love   whatever it was I did to you.

1920

To Mayakovsky

High above cross and trumpet
baptised in smoke and fire
my clumsy-footed angel –
Hello there, Vladimir!

Carter and horse at once
justice and whim together.
He used to spit on his palms –
Hold on, carthorse of glory!

Singer of gutter miracles,
grubby, arrogant friend –
Hullo there, you who prefer
topaz to diamond!

Now yawn, play your trump card
my thunderbolt of cobbles,
and rake this horse's shaft
once more with your angel wing.

1921

Praise to the Rich

And so, making clear in advance
I know there are miles   between us;
and I reckon myself with the tramps, which
is a place of honour in this world:

under the wheels of luxury, at
table with cripples and hunchbacks ...
From the top of the bell-tower roof,
I proclaim it: I *love* the rich.

For their rotten, unsteady root
for the damage done in their cradle
for the absent-minded way their hands
go in and out of their pockets;

for the way their softest word is
obeyed like a shouted order; because
they will not be let into heaven; and
because they don't look in your eyes;

and because they send secrets   by courier!
and their passions   by errand boy.
In the nights that are thrust upon them they
kiss and drink under compulsion,

and because in all their accountings
in boredom, in gilding, in wadding,
they can't buy me   I'm too brazen:
I confirm it, I *love* the rich!

and in spite of their shaven fatness,
their fine drink   (wink, and spend):
some sudden   defeatedness
and a look that is like a dog's

doubting...
                    the core of their balance
nought, but are the weights true?
I say that among all outcasts
there are no such orphans on earth.

There is also a nasty fable
about camels getting through needles
      for that look, surprised to death
apologizing for sickness, as

if they were suddenly bankrupt: 'I would have been
glad to lend, but'   and their silence.
'I counted in carats once and then I was one of them.'
For all these things, I swear it: I *love* the rich.

1922

God help us   Smoke!

God help us   Smoke!
   – Forget that. Look at the damp.
These are the ordinary fears
   of anyone moving house

approaching a poor lamp
   for students in miserable outskirts.:
– Isn't there even a tree
   for the children? What sort of landlord

will we have? Too strict?
   in a necklace of coins, a porter
impervious as: fate
   to the shudder in our pockets.

What kind of neighbour?
   Unmarried? Perhaps not noisy?
The old place was no pleasure
   but still the air there breathed

our atmosphere, was soaked
   in our own odours. Easy,
to put up with fetid air
   if it isn't soiled by outsiders!

It was old, of course, and
   rotting, but still … Not a hostel room!
I don't know about being born
   but this is for dying in!

1922

Ophelia: in Defence of the Queen

Prince, let's have no more disturbing
 these wormy flower-beds. Look at
the living rose, and think of a woman
 snatching a single day – from the few left to her.

Prince Hamlet, you defile the Queen's
 womb. Enough. A virgin cannot
judge passion. Don't you know Phaedra
 was more guilty, yet men still sing of her,

and will go on singing. You, with your blend
 of chalk and rot, you bony
scandalmonger, how can you ever
 understand a fever in the blood?

Beware, if you continue … I can
 rise up through flagstones into the grand bed-chamber
of so much sweetness, I myself, to defend her.
 I myself – your own undying passion!

1923

Wherever you are I can reach you

Wherever you are I can reach you
to summon up – or send you back again!
Yet I'm no sorceress. My eyes grew sharp in
the white book – of that far-off river Don.

From the height of my cedar I see a world
where court decisions float, and all lights wander.
Yet from here I can turn the whole sea upside down
to bring you from its depths or send you under!

You can't resist me, since I'm everywhere:
at daylight, underground, in breath and bread,
I'm always present. That is how I shall procure
your lips – as God will surely claim your soul –

in your last breath – and even in that choking hour
I'll be there, at the great Archangel's fence,
to put these bloodied lips against the thorns
of Judgement – and to snatch you from your bier!

Give in! You must. This is no fairytale.
Give in! Any arrow will fall back on you.
Give in! Don't you know no one escapes
the power of creatures reaching out with

breath alone? (That's how I soar up
with my eyes shut and mica round my mouth…)
Careful, the prophetess tricked Samuel.
Perhaps I'll hoodwink you. Return alone,

because another girl is with you. Now on Judgement Day
there'll be no litigation. So till then
I'll go on wandering.
               And yet I'll have your soul
as an alchemist knows how to win your

Lips …

                                            1923

From *Wires*

1

Along these singing lines that run
from pole to pole, supporting heaven,
I send along to you my portion
of earthly dust.
                     From wires
to poles. This alley sighs
the telegraphic words: I lo-o-ve …

I beg. (No printed form would
hold that word! But wires are simpler.)
Atlas himself upon these poles
lowered the racetrack
of the Gods.
                        Along these files
the telegraphic word: g-oo-oodbye …

Do you hear it? This last word
torn from my hoarse throat: Forg-i-ive …
Over these calm Atlantic fields
the rigging holds. And higher, higher,
all the messages fuse together
in Ariadne's web: Retu-u-rn …
And plaintive cries of: I won't leave …

These wires are steely guards upon
voices from Hell,

receding … far into that distance,
still implored for some compassion.

Compassion? (But in such a chorus
can you distinguish such a noise?)
That cry, arising as death comes –
through mounds – and ditches – that last
waft of her – passion that persists –
Euridice's: A-a-alas,

and not – a –

                                                    1923

                    7

Patiently, as tarmac under hammers,
patiently, as what is new matures,
patiently, as death must be awaited,
patiently, as vengeance may be nursed –

So I shall wait for you. (One look down to earth.
Cobblestones. Lips between teeth. And numb.)
Patiently, as sloth can be prolonged,
patiently, as someone threading beads.

Toboggans squeak outside; the door answers.
Now the wind's roar is inside the forest.
What has arrived is writing, whose corrections
are lofty as a change of reign, or a prince's entrance.

And let's go home!
this is inhuman –
Yet it's mine.

1923

Sahara

Young men, don't ride away! Sand
    stifled the soul of the
last one to disappear and now
    he's altogether dumb.

To look for him is useless.
    (Young men, I never lie.)
That lost one now reposes
    in a reliable grave.

He once rode into me as if
    through lands of
miracles and fire, with all
    the power of poetry, and

I was: dry, sandy, without day.
    He used poetry
to invade my depths, like chose of
    any other country!

Listen to this story of two
    souls, without jealousy:
we entered one another's eyes
    as if they were oases –

I took him into me as if he were
    a god, in passion,
simply because of a charming tremor
    in his young throat.

Without a name he sank into me. But now
    he's gone. Don't search for him.
All deserts forget the thousands of
    those who sleep in them.

And afterwards the Sahara in one
    seething collapse will
cover you also with sand like sprinkled
    foam. And be your hill!

1923

The Poet

1

A poet's speech begins   a great way off.
A poet is   carried far away by speech

by way of planets, signs, and the ruts
of roundabout parables, between *yes* and *no,*
in his hands even sweeping gestures from a bell-tower
become hook-like. For the way of comets

is the poet's way. And the blown-apart
links of causality   are his links. Look up
after him without hope. The eclipses of
poets are not foretold in the calendar.

He is the one that mixes up the cards
and confuses   arithmetic and weight,
demands answers from the school bench,
the one who altogether refutes Kant,

the one in the stone graves of the Bastille
who remains like a tree in its loveliness.
And yet the one whose   traces have always vanished,
the train everyone always arrives
too late to catch

                    for the path of comets
is the path of poets: they burn without warming,
pick without cultivating. They are: an explosion, a breaking in –
and the mane of their path makes the   curve of a
graph   cannot be foretold by the calendar.

                    2

    There are superfluous people about in
    this world, out of sight, who
    aren't listed in any directory; and
    home for them is   a rubbish heap.

    They are hollow, jostled creatures:
    who keep silent, dumb as dung, they are
    nails   catching in your silken hem
    dirt   imagined under your wheels.

    Here they are, ghostly and invisible, the
    sign is on them, like the speck of the leper.
    People like Job in this world who
    might even have envied him. If.

    We are poets, which has the sound of outcast.
    Nevertheless, we step out from our shores.
    We dare contend for godhead, with goddesses,
    and for the Virgin   with the gods themselves.

3

Now what shall I do here, blind and fatherless?
Everyone else can see and has a father.
Passion in this world has to leap anathema
as it might be over the walls of a trench
and weeping   is called a cold in the head.

What shall I do, by nature and trade
a singing creature (like a wire – sunburn! Siberia!)
as I go over the bridge of my enchanted
visions, that cannot be weighed, in a
world that deals only in weights and measures?

What shall I do, singer and first-born, in a
world where the deepest black is grey,
and inspiration is kept in   a thermos?
with all this immensity
in a measured world?

1923

Appointment

I'll be late for the meeting
we arranged. When I arrive, my hair
will be grey. Yes, I suppose I grabbed
at Spring. And you set your hopes much too high.

I shall walk with this bitterness for years
across mountains or town squares equally,
(Ophelia didn't flinch at rue!) I'll walk
on souls and on hands without shuddering.

Living on. As the earth continues.
With blood in every thicket, every creek.
Even though Ophelia's face is waiting
between the grasses bordering every stream.

She gulped at love, and filled her mouth
with silt. A shaft of light on metal!
I set my love upon you. Much too high.
In the sky   arrange my burial.

1923

Rails

The bed of a railway cutting
   has tidy sheets. The steel-blue
parallel tracks ruled out
   as needy as staves of music.

And over them people are driven
   like possessed creatures from Pushkin
whose piteous song   has been silenced.
   Look, they're departing, deserting.

And yet lag behind: and linger,
   the note of pain always rising
higher than love, as the poles freeze
   to the bank, like Lot's wife, forever.

Despair has appointed an hour for me
   (as someone arranges a marriage): then
Sappho with her voice gone
   I shall weep like a simple seamstress

with a cry of passive lament —
   a marsh heron! The moving train
will hoot its way over the sleepers
   and slice through them like scissors.

Colours blur in my eye,
   their glow a meaningless red.
All young women at times
   are tempted — by such a bed!

1923

You loved me

You loved me. And your lies had their own probity.
  There was a truth in every falsehood.
Your love went far beyond any possible
  boundary   as no one else's could.

Your love seemed to last even longer
  than time itself. Now you wave your hand
and suddenly your   love for me is over!
  That is the truth in five words.

1923

It's not like waiting for post

It's not like waiting for post.
This is how you wait for
the one letter you need:
soft stuff bound with
tape and paste.
Inside a little word.
That's all. Happiness.

Waiting for happiness?
It's more like waiting for death.
The soldiers will salute
and three chunks of lead
will slam into your chest.
Your eyes will then flash red.

No question of joy.
Too old now, all bloom gone.
Waiting for what else now but
black muzzles in a square yard.

A square letter. I think
there may be spells in the ink.
No hope. And no one is
too old to face death

or such a square envelope.

1923

My ear attends to you

My ear attends to you,
as a mother hears in her sleep.
To a feverish child, she whispers
as I bend over you.

At the skin, my blood calls out to
your heart, my whole sky craves
an island of tenderness.
My rivers tilt towards you.

And I am drawn downwards
as stairs slope into a garden,
or some willow's bough falls
straight down, away from the milestone.

Stars are pulled to the earth
and laurels on graves won
with suffering, attract banners.
An owl longs for a hollow.

And I lean down
towards you with muscle and wing,
as if to a grave stone,
(I put the years to sleep)

my lips seek yours ... like spring.

1923

As people listen intently

As people listen intently
    (a river's mouth to its source)
that's how they smell a flower
to the depths, till they lose all sense.

That's how they feel their deepest
    craving in dark air,
as children lying in blue sheets
peer into memory.

And that's how a young boy feels
when his blood begins to change.
    When people fall in love with love
they fling themselves in the abyss.

1923

Strong doesn't mate with strong

Strong doesn't mate with strong.
It's not allowed in this world.
So Siegfried missed Brunhilde,
in marriage fixed by a sword.

Like buffaloes, stone on stone,
in brotherly hatred joined,
he left their marriage bed, unknown,
she slept, unrecognised.

Apart, in the marriage bed.
Apart, in ambiguous language.
Apart, and clutched like a fist.
Too late.   And apart.   That's marriage.

More ancient evil yet:
Achilles, Thetis' son
crushing the Amazon
like a lion, missed Penthesilea.

Think of her glance, when felled
from her horse in the mud,
she looked up at him then
and not down from Olympus.

And afterwards, his passion was
to snatch his wife back from darkness?
But equal never mates with equal.

And so, we missed each other.

1924

In a world

In a world where most people
are hunched and sweaty:
I know only one person
equal to me in strength.

In a world where there is
so much to want
I know only one person
equal to me in power.

In a world where mould
and ivy cover everything
I know only one person – you –
who equals me in spirit.

1924

Poem of the Mountain

Liebster, Dich wundert
die Rede? Alle Scheidenden
reden wie Trunkene und
nehmen sich festlich …
                    – Hölderlin

A shudder: off my shoulders
    with this mountain! My soul rises.
Now let me sing of sorrow which
    is my own mountain

a blackness which I will
    never block out again:
Let me sing of sorrow
    from the top of the mountain!

1

A mountain, like the body of
a recruit mown down by shells,
wanting lips that were
unkissed, and a wedding ceremony

the mountain demanded those.
Instead, an ocean broke into its ears
with sudden shouts of hooray! Though
the mountain fought and struggled.

The mountain was like thunder!
A chest drummed on by Titans.
(Do you remember that last house
of the mountain – the end of the suburb?)

The mountain was many worlds!
And God took a high price for one.
Sorrow began with a mountain.
This mountain looked on the town.

2

Not Parnassus   not Sinai
simply a bare and military
hill. Form up! Fire!
Why is it then in my eyes
(since it was October and not May)
that mountain was Paradise?

3

On an open hand Paradise was offered,
(if it's too hot, don't even touch it!)
threw itself under our feet with all
its gullies and steep crags,

with paws of Titans, with all
its shrubbery and pines
the mountain seized the skirts of our
coats, and commanded: stop.

How far from schoolbook Paradise
it was: so *windy,* when
the mountain pulled us down on our
backs. To itself. Saying: lie here!

The violence of that pull bewildered us.
How? Even now I don't know.
Mountain. Pimp. For holiness.
It pointed, to say: here.

4

How to forget Persephone's pomegranate
grain in the coldness of winter?
I remember lips half-opening to
mine, like the valves of a shell-creature

lost because of that grain, Persephone!
Continuous as the redness of lips,
and your eyelashes   were like jagged points
upon the golden angles of a star.

5

Not that passion is   deceitful or imaginary!
It doesn't lie. Simply, it doesn't last!
If only we could come into this world as though
we were common people in love

be sensible, see things as they are: this
is just a hill, just a bump in the ground.
(And yet they say it is by the pull of
abysses, that you measure height.)

In the heaps of gorse, coloured dim
among islands of tortured pines ...
(In delirium above the level of
life)
        – Take me then. I'm yours.

Instead only the gentle mercies of
domesticity – chicks twittering –
because we came down into this world who
once lived at the height of heaven: in love.

6

The mountain was mourning (and mountains do mourn,
their clay is bitter, in the hours of parting).
The mountain mourned: for the tenderness
(like doves) of our undiscovered mornings.

The mountain mourned: for our friendliness, for
that unbreakable kinship of the lips.
The mountain declared that everyone will
receive in proportion to his tears.

The mountain grieved because   life is a gypsy-camp,
and we go marketing all our life from heart to heart.
And this was Hagar's grief. To be
sent far away. Even with her child.

Also the mountain said that all things were a trick
of some demon, no sense to the game.
The mountain sorrowed. And we were silent,
leaving the mountain to judge the case.

7

The mountain mourned for what is now blood
and heat will turn only to sadness.
The mountain mourned. It will not let us go.
It will not let you lie with someone else!

The mountain mourned, for what is now
world and Rome will turn   only to smoke.
The mountain mourned, because we shall be with
others. (And I do not envy them!)

The mountain mourned: for the terrible load
of promises, too late for us to renounce.
The mountain mourned the ancient nature of
the Gordian knot of law and passion.

The mountain mourned for our mourning also.
For tomorrow! Not yet! Above our foreheads
will break – death's sea of – memories!
For tomorrow, when we shall realise!

That sound   what?   as if someone were
crying just nearby? Can that be it?
The mountain is mourning. Because we must go down
separately, over such mud,

into life which we all know is nothing but
mob market barracks:
That sound said: all poems of
mountains   are written   *thus*

8

Hump of Atlas, groaning
   Titan, this town where we
live, day in, day out, will come
   to take a pride in the mountain

where we defeated life – at cards, and
   insisted with passion *not to*
exist. Like a bear-pit.
   And the twelve apostles.

Pay homage to my dark cave,
   (I was a cave that the waves entered).
The last hand of the card game was
   played, you remember, at the edge of the suburb?

Mountain   many worlds   the
   gods take revenge on their own likeness!

And my grief began with this mountain
which sits above me now like my headstone.

9

Years will pass. And then   the inscribed
slab will be changed for tombstone and removed.
There will be summerhouses on our mountain.
Soon it will be hemmed in with gardens,

because in outskirts like this they say
the air is better, and it's easier to live:
so it will be cut into plots of land,
and many lines of scaffolding will cross it.

They will straighten my mountain passes.
All my ravines will be upended.
There must be people who want to bring happiness
into their *home,* to have *happiness.*

Happiness at home! Love without fiction.
Imagine: without any stretching of sinews.
I have to be a woman   and endure this!
(There was happiness – when you used to come,

happiness – in my home.) Love without any extra
sweetness given by parting. Or a knife.
Now on the ruins of our happiness
a town will grow: of husbands and wives.

And in that same blessed air, while
you can, everyone   should sin –
soon shopkeepers on holidays
will be chewing the cud of their profits,

thinking out new levels and corridors, as
everything leads them back   to their house!
For there has to be someone who needs
a roof with a stork's nest!

10

Yet under the weight of these foundations
the mountain will not forget   the game.
Though people go astray   they must remember.
And the mountain has   mountains of time.

Obstinate crevices and cracks remain;
in summer homes, they'll realise, too late,
this is no hill, overgrown with families, but
a volcano! Make money out of that!

Can vineyards ever hold the danger
of Vesuvius? A giant without fear cannot
be bound with flax. And the delirium
of lips alone has   the same power:

to make the vineyards stir and turn heavily,
to belch out their lava of hate.
Your daughters shall all become prostitutes
and all your sons turn into   poets!

You shall rear a bastard child, my daughter!
Waste your flesh upon the gypsies, son!
May you never own a piece of fertile land
you   who take your substance from my blood.

Harder than any cornerstone, as
binding as the words of a dying man,
I curse you: do not look for happiness
upon my mountain   where you move like ants!

At some hour unforeseen, some time unknowable,
you will realise, the whole lot of you, how
enormous and without measure is
the mountain of God's seventh law.

Epilogue

There are blanks in memory   cataracts
on our eyes; the seven veils.
I no longer remember you separately
as a face but a white emptiness

without true features. All – is a
whiteness. (My spirit is one
uninterrupted wound.) The chalk of
details must   belong to tailors!

The dome of heaven was   built in a single frame
and oceans   are featureless   a mass of
drops that cannot be distinguished. You
are unique. And love is no detective.

Let now some neighbour say whether your
hair is black or fair, for he can tell.
I leave that to physicians or watchmakers.
What passion has a use for such details?

You are a full, unbroken circle, a
whirlwind or   wholly turned to stone.
I cannot think of you apart from
love. There is an   equals sign.

(In heaps of sleepy down, and falls of
water, hills of foam, there is
a new sound, strange to my hearing,
instead of I   a regal *we)*

and though life's beggared now and
narrowed into   how things are
still I cannot see you joined to
anyone: a
            revenge of memory.

                              finished 1 Dec 1924

Poem of the End

1

A single post, a point of rusting
     tin in the sky
marks the fated place we
     move to, he and I

on time   as death is
     prompt   strangely
too smooth the gesture of
     his hat to me

menace at the edges of his
     eyes   his mouth tight
shut   strangely too low is the
     bow he makes tonight

on time?   that false note in
          his voice, what
is it the brain alerts to and the
          heart drops at?

under that evil sky, that sign of
          tin and rust.
Six o'clock. There he is waiting
          by the post.

Now we kiss soundlessly, his
          lips stiff as
hands are given to queens, or
          dead people thus

round us the shoving elbows of
          ordinary bustle
and strangely irksome rises the
          screech of a whistle

howls like a dog screaming
          angrier, longer: what
a nightmare strangeness life is
          at death point

and that nightmare reached my waist
          only last night
and now reaches the stars, it has
          grown to its true height

crying silently love love until
          – Has it gone
six, shall we go to the cinema?
          I shout it: home!

And what have we come to?
   tents of nomads
thunder and drawn swords over
   our heads, some

terror we expect
   listen   houses
collapsing in the one
   word: home.

It is   the whine of a cossetted
   child lost, it is the
noise a baby makes for
   give and *mine.*

Brother in dissipation, cause
   of this cold fever, you
hurry now to get home just
   as men rush in leaving

like a horse jerking the
   line   rope down in the dust.
Is there even a building there?
   Ten steps before us.

A house on the hill   no higher   a
   house on the top of the hill and
a window under the roof   *is it*
   from the red sun alone

it is burning?   or is it my life
   which must begin again? how
simple poems are: it means I
   must go out into the night
              and talk to

who shall I tell my sorrow
   my horror greener than ice?
– You've been thinking too much.
   A solemn answer: yes.

3

And the embankment   I hold
      to water   thick and solid as
if we had come to the hanging
      gardens of Semiramis

to water   a strip as colourless
      as a slab for corpses
I am like a female singer holding
      to her music. To this wall.

Blindly   for you won't return
      or listen, even if I bend to
the quencher of all thirst, I am
hanging at the gutter of a roof.

Lunatic. It is not the river
      (I was born naiad) that makes me
shiver now, she was a hand I held
      to, when you walked beside me, a lover

and faithful.
                    The dead are faithful
though not to all in their cells; if
      death lies on my left now,
it is at your side I feel it.

Now a shaft of astonishing light, and
      laughter   that cheap tambourine.
– You and I must   have a talk. And
      I shiver: let's be brave, shall we?

TRANSLATIONS – *Marina Tsvetayeva*   261

A blonde mist, a wave of
gauze ruffles, of human
breathing, smoky exhalations
endless talk   the smell of
what? of haste and filth
connivance   shabby acts   all
the secrets of business men
      and ballroom powder.

Family men   like bachelors
move in their rings like middle-aged boys
always joking   always laughing, and
calculating, always calculating
large deals   and little ones, they are
snout-deep in the feathers of some
business arrangement
      and ballroom powder.

(I am half-turned away   is this
our house? I am not mistress here)
Someone   over his cheque book
another bends to a kid glove hand
a third works at a delicate foot
in patent leather   furtively   the smell
rises of marriage-broking
      and ballroom powder.

In the window is the silver
bite of a tooth: it is the Star of Malta,
which is the sign of stroking, of the love
that leads to pawing and to pinching.
(Yesterday's food perhaps   but
nobody worries if it smells slightly)
      of dirt, commercial tricks
      and ballroom powder.

The chain is too short perhaps even
it is not steel but platinum?
Look how their three chins shake
like cows munching their own veal
above their sugared necks
the devils swing on a gas lamp
    smelling of business slumps
and another powder
made by Berthold Schwartz
                              genius
intercessor for people:
— You and I must   have a talk
    — Let's be brave, shall we?

5

I catch a movement of his
    lips, but he won't
speak — You don't   love me?
    — Yes, but in torment

drained and driven to death
    (He looks round like an eagle)
— You call this   home? It's
    in the heart. — What *literature!*

For love is flesh, it is a
    flower flooded with blood.
Did you think it was just a
    little chat across a table

a snatched hour and back home again
    the way gentlemen and ladies
play at it? Either love is
— A shrine?
                    — or else a scar.

A scar   every servant and guest
    can see (and I think silently:
love is a bow-string pulled
    back to the point of breaking).

TRANSLATIONS — *Marina Tsvetayeva*   263

Love is a bond. That has snapped for
    us   our mouths and lives part
(I begged you not to put a
    spell on me that holy hour

close on mountain heights of
    passion   memory is mist).
Yes, love is a matter of gifts
    thrown in the fire, for nothing

The shell-fish crack of his mouth
    is pale, no chance of a smile:
— Love is a large bed.
    — Or else an empty gulf.

Now his fingers begin to
    beat, no mountains
move. Love is —
                — *Mine:* yes.
I understand. And so?

The drum beat of his fingers
    grows (scaffold and square)
— Let's go, he says. For me, let's
    die, would be easier.

Enough cheap stuff   rhymes
    like railway hotel rooms, so:
— love means life   although
    the ancients had a different

name.
        — Well?
                    — A scrap
of handkerchief in a fist
like a fish. Shall we go? How,
    bullet   rail   poison

death anyway, choose: I make no
    plans. A Roman, you
survey the men still alive
    like an eagle:
                    say goodbye.

6

I didn't want this, not
   this (but listen, quietly,
to want is what bodies do
   and now we are ghosts only).

And yet I   didn't say it
   though the time of the train is set
and the sorrowful honour of leaving
   is a cup given to women

or perhaps in madness I
   misheard you   polite liar:
is this the bouquet that you give your
   love, this blood-stained honour?

Is it? Sound follows
   sound clearly: was it goodbye
you said? (as sweetly casual
   as a handkerchief dropped without

thought) in this battle
   you are Caesar (What an
insolent thrust, to put the
   weapon of defeat, into my hand

like a trophy). It continues. To
   sound in my ears. As I bow.
– Do you always pretend
   to be forestalled in breaking?

Don't deny this, it
   is a vengeance of Lovelace
a gesture that does you credit
   while it lifts the flesh

from my bones. Laughter   the laugh of
   death. Moving. Without desire.
That is for others now
   we are shadows to one another.

Hammer the last nail in
  screw up the lead coffin.
— And now a last request.
    — Of course. — Then say nothing

about us   to those who will
    come after me. (The sick
on their stretchers talk of spring.)
— May I ask the same thing?

Perhaps I should give you a ring?
    — No. Your look is no longer open.
The stamp left on your heart
    would be the ring on your hand.

So now   without any scenes
    I must swallow, silently, furtively.
— A book then? — No, you give those
    to everyone, don't even write them

    books …

So now   must   be no
so now   must   be no
must be no crying

In wandering tribes of
fishermen brothers
drink without crying

dance without crying
their blood is hot, they
pay without crying

pearls in a glass
melt, as they run their
world   without crying

            Now I am going and this
            Harlequin gives his
            Pierrette a bone like
            a piece of contempt

He throws her the honour
of ending the curtain, the last
word when one inch of lead in
the breast would be hotter and better

Cleaner. My   teeth
press my lips. I can
stop myself crying

pressing the sharpness
into the softest
so without crying

so tribes of nomads
die without crying
burn without crying.

So tribes of fishermen
in ash and song can
hide their dead man.

7

And the embankment. The last one.
        Finished. Separate, and hands apart
like neighbours avoiding one another. We
        walk away from the river, from my

cries. Falling salts of mercury
        I lick off without attention.
No great moon of Solomon
        has been set for my tears in the skies.

A post. Why not beat my forehead to
        blood on it? To smithereens! We are
like fellow criminals, fearing one
        another. (The murdered thing is love.)

Don't say these are lovers? Going into
        the night? Separately? To sleep with others?
You understand the future is up there?
        he says. And I throw back my head.

To sleep! Like newly-weds over their mat!
    To sleep! We can't fall into
step. And I plead miserably: take my
    arm, we aren't convicts to walk like this.

Shock! It's as though his *soul* has touched
    me   as his arm leans on mine. The electric
current beats along feverish wiring,
    and rips. He's leaned on my soul with his arm.

He holds me. Rainbows everywhere. What is more like a
    rainbow than tears? Rain, a curtain, denser
than beads. I don't know if such embankments can
    end. But here is a bridge and
                              – Well then?

Here? (The hearse is ready.)
    Peaceful   his eyes move
upward. Couldn't you see me home
    for the very last time?

                    8

            Last   bridge   I won't
            give up or take out my hand
            this is the last bridge
            the last bridging between

            water   and firm land:
            and I am saving these
            coins for death
            for Charon, the price of Lethe

            this   shadow money
            from my dark hand I press
            soundlessly into
            the shadowy darkness of his

            shadow money it is
            no gleam and tinkle in it
            coins for shadows:
            the dead have enough poppies

This bridge

Lovers for the most
part are without hope: passion
also is just
a bridge, a means of connection

It's warm: to nestle
close at your ribs, to move in
a visionary pause
towards nothing, beside nothing

no   arms no   legs
now, only the bone of my
side is alive where
it presses directly against you

life in that side
only, ear and echo is it: there
I stick like white to
egg yolk, or an eskimo to his fur

adhesive, pressing
joined to you: Siamese
twins are no nearer.
The woman you call mother

when she forgot
all things in motionless triumph
only to carry you:
she did not hold you closer.

Understand: we have
grown into one as we slept and
now I can't jump
because I can't let go your hand

and I won't be torn off
as I press close to you: this
bridge is no husband
but a lover: a just slipping past

our support: for the
river is fed with bodies!
I bite in like a tick
you must tear out my roots to be rid of me

like ivy   like a tick
inhuman   godless
to throw me away like a thing,
when there is

no thing I ever prized
in this empty world of things.
Say this is only dream,
night still and afterwards morning

an express   to Rome?
Granada? I won't know myself
as I push off
the Himalayas of bedclothes.

But this dark is deep:
now I warm you with my blood, listen
to this flesh.
It is far truer than poems.

If you are warm, who
will you go to tomorrow for that?
This is delirium,
please say this bridge cannot

end
          as it ends.

– Here then? His gesture could
be made by a child, or a god.
– And so? – I am biting in!
For a little more time. The last of it.

9

Blatant as factory buildings,
    as alert to a call
here is the sacred and sublingual
    secret wives keep from husbands and

widows from friends, here is the full
    story that Eve took from the tree:
I am no more than an animal that
    someone has stabbed in the stomach.

Burning. As if the soul had been
    torn away with the skin. Vanished like steam
through a hole is that well-known foolish
    heresy called a soul.

That Christian leprosy:
    steam: save that with your poultices.
There never was such a thing.
    There was a body once, wanted to

live   no longer wants to live.

Forgive me! I didn't mean it!
    The shriek of torn entrails.
So prisoners sentenced to death wait
    for the 4 a.m. firing squad.

At chess perhaps with a grin
    they mock the corridor's eye.
Pawns in the game of chess:
    someone is playing with us.

Who? Kind gods or? Thieves?
    The peephole is filled with an
eye   and the red corridor
    clanks. Listen   the latch lifts.

One drag on tobacco, then
    spit, it's all over, spit,
along this paving of chess squares
    is a direct path   to the ditch

to blood. And the secret eye
the dormer eye of the moon.

And now, squinting sideways, how
far away you are already.

10

Closely, like one creature, we
start: there is our café!

There is our island, our shrine, where
in the morning, we people of the

rabble, a couple for a minute only,
conducted a morning service:

with things from country markets, sour
things seen through sleep or   spring.
The coffee was nasty there
entirely made from oats (and

with oats you can extinguish
caprice in fine race-horses).
There was no smell of Araby.
Arcadia was in

that coffee.

But how *she* smiled at us
and sat us down by her,
sad and worldly in her wisdom
a grey-haired paramour.

Her smile was solicitous
(saying: you'll wither! live!),
it was a smile at madness and being
penniless, at yawns   and love

and – this was the chief thing –
at laughter   without reason
smiles   with no deliberation
and our faces   without wrinkles.

Most of all   at youth
at passions   out of this climate
blown in from some other place
flowing from some other source

into that dim café
(burnous and Tunis) where
she smiled at hope and flesh
under old-fashioned clothes.

(My dear friend   I don't complain.
It's just another scar.)
To think how she saw us off,
that proprietress in her cap

stiff   as a Dutch hat ...

Not quite remembering, not quite
understanding, we are led away from the festival –
along our street!   no longer ours   that
we walked many times, and no more shall.

Tomorrow the sun will rise in the West.
And then David will break with Jehovah.
– What are we doing? – We are *separating*.
– That's a word that means nothing to me.

It's the most inhumanly senseless
of words: *sep   arating*. (Am I one of a hundred?)
It is simply a word of four syllables and
behind their sound lies: emptiness.

Wait! Is it even correct in Serbian or
Croatian? Is it a Czech whim, this word.
Sep   aration! To *sep   arate!*
It is insane   unnatural

a sound to burst the eardrums, and spread out
far beyond the limits of longing itself.
Separation – the word is not in the Russian
language. Or the language of women. Or men.

Nor in the language of God. What are we – sheep?
To stare about us as we eat.
Separation – in what language is it,
when the meaning itself doesn't exist?

or even the sound! Well – an empty one, like
the noise of a saw in your sleep perhaps.
Separation. That belongs to the school of
Khlebuikov's   nightingale-groaning

swan-like …
                    so how does it happen?
Like a lake of water running dry.
Into air. I can feel our hands touching.
To separate. Is a shock of thunder

upon my head – oceans rushing into
a wooden house. This is Oceania's
furthest promontory. And the streets are steep.
To separate. That means to go downward

downhill   the sighing sound of two
heavy soles   and at last a hand receives
the nail in it.   A logic that turns
everything over. *To separate*

means we have to become
single creatures   again

we who had grown into one.

12

Dense as a horse mane is:
        rain in our eyes. And hills.
We have passed the suburb.
        Now we are out of town,

    which is there   but not for us.
        Stepmother   not mother.
    Nowhere   is lying ahead.
        And here   is where we fall.

A field with. A fence and.
    Brother and sister. Standing.
Life is   only a suburb:
    so you must build elsewhere.

Ugh, what a lost cause
    it is, ladies and: gentlemen,
for the whole world   is suburb:
    Where   are the real towns?

Rain rips at us madly.
    We stand and break with each other.
In three months, these must be
    the first moments of sharing.

Is it true, God, that you even
    tried to borrow from Job?
Well, it didn't come off.
    Still. We are. Outside town.

Beyond it! Understand? Outside!
    That means   we've passed the walls.
Life is a place where it's forbidden
    to live. Like the Hebrew quarter.

And isn't it more worthy to
    become an eternal Jew?
Anyone not   a reptile
    suffers the same pogrom.

Life is for converts only
    Judases of all faiths.
Let's go to leprous islands
    or hell   anywhere   only not

life   which puts up with traitors, with
    those who are sheep   to butchers!
This paper which gives me the
    right to live – I stamp. With my feet.:

Stamp! for the shield of David.
    Vengeance! for heaps of bodies
and they say after all (delicious) the
    Jews didn't want to live!

Ghetto of the chosen. Beyond this
    ditch. No mercy:
In this   most Christian of worlds
    all poets   are Jews.

13

This is how they sharpen knives on a
    stone, and sweep sawdust up with
brooms. Under my hands there is
    something wet and furry.

Now where are those twin male
    virtues: strength, dryness?:
Here beneath my hand I can
    feel   tears. Not rain!

What temptations can still be
    spoken of? Property is   water.
Since l felt your diamond eyes under
    my hands, flowing.

There is no more I can lose. We have
    reached the end of ending.
And so I simply stroke, and
    stroke. And stroke your face.

This is the kind of pride we have:
    Marinkas   are Polish girls.
Since now the eyes of an eagle weep
    underneath these hands ...

Can you be crying? My friend, my
    – everything! Please forgive me!
How large and salty now is the
    taste of that in my fist.

Male tears are – cruel! They
    rise over my head! Weep,
there will soon be others to
    heal any guilt towards me.

Fish of   identic-
    al sea. A sweep upward! like
... any dead shells and any
    lips upon lips.

In tears.
Wormwood
to taste.
– And tomorrow
when
I am awake?

14

A slope like a path   for
sheep. With town noises.
Three trollops approaching
They are laughing. At tears.

They are laughing   the full noon of
their bellies shake, like waves!
They laugh at the
                            inappropriate
disgraceful, male

tears of yours, visible
through the rain   like scars!
Like a shameful   pearl on
the bronze of a warrior.

These first and last tears
pour them now – for me –
for your tears   are pearls
that I wear in my crown.

And my eyes are not lowered.
I stare through   the shower.
Yes, dolls of Venus
stare at me! because

This is a closer bond
than the transport of lying down.
The Song of Songs itself
gives place to our speech,

infamous birds as we are
Solomon bows to us, for
our simultaneous cries
are   something more than a dream!

And into the hollow waves of
darkness – hunched and level –
without trace – in silence –
something sinks like a ship.

                                                        1924

An Attempt at Jealousy

How is your life with the other one,
       simpler, isn't it? One   stroke of the oar
then a long coastline, and soon
       even the memory of me

will be a floating island
       (in the sky, not on the waters):
spirits, spirits, you will be
       sisters, and never lovers.

How is your life with an ordinary
       woman?   without godhead?
Now that your sovereign has
       been deposed (and you have stepped down).

How is your life? Are you fussing?
       flinching? How   do you get up?
The tax of deathless vulgarity
       can you cope with it, poor man?

'Scenes and hysterics   I've had
   enough! I'll rent my own house.'
How is your life with the other one
   now, you that I chose for my own?

More to your taste, more delicious
   is it, your food? Don't moan if you sicken.
How is your life with an *image*
   you, who walked on Sinai?

How is your life with a stranger
   from this world? Can you (be frank)
love her? Or do you   feel shame
   like Zeus' reins on your forehead?

How is your life? Are you
   healthy? How do you   sing?
How do you deal with the pain
   of an undying conscience, poor man?

How is your life with a piece of market
   stuff, at a steep price.
After Carrara marble,
   how is your life with the dust of

plaster now? (God was hewn from
   stone, but he is smashed to bits.)
How do you live with one of a
   thousand women   after Lilith?

Sated with newness, are you?
   Now you are grown cold to magic,
how is your life with an
   earthly woman, without a sixth

sense? Tell me: are you happy?
   Not? In a shallow pit How is
your life, my love? Is it as
   hard as mine with another man?

1924

To Boris Pasternak

Distance: versts, miles ...
divide us; they've dispersed us,
to make us behave quietly
at our different ends of the earth.

Distance: how many miles of it
lie between us now – disconnected –
crucified – then dissected.
And they don't know – it unites us.

Our spirits and sinews fuse,
there's no discord between us.
though our separated pieces
                          lie outside
the moat – for eagles!

This conspiracy of miles
has not yet disconcerted us,
however much they've pushed us, like
orphans into backwaters.

– What then? Well. Now it's March!
And we're scattered like some pack of cards!

1925

From *The Ratcatcher*

From Chapter 1

Hamelin, the good-mannered
    town of window-boxes,
well-stocked with
    warehouses
              Paradise Town!

How God must love
    these sensible
townspeople. Every one
    is righteous:

Goody-goody, always-right, always-provided-for,
stocked-up-in-time. It's Paradise Town!

Here are no riddles.
    All is smooth and peaceable.
Only good habits in
                Paradise
                Town.

In God's sweet
    backwater
(The Devil turns his
    nose up here):

It's goody-goody Paradise (owned by Schmidt and Mayers).
A town for an Emperor. Give way to your elders!

Everywhere is tranquil.
    No fire. The whole place
must belong to Abel.
    Isn't that
                Paradise?

Those who are not
    too cold or too hot
travel straight to Hamelin
    straight into Hamelin:

Lullaby and ermine-down, this is Paradise Town!
Everywhere is good advice and go-to-sleep on time Town!
First watch!
First watch!
With the world all contact's lost!
Is the dog out? And the cat in?
Did you hear the early warning.

Take your servants out of harness
   Shake your pipe – you've time for that –
but leave your workbench now because
   'Morgen ist auch ein tag'

Ten to ten!
Ten to ten.
Put your woolly earplugs in.
In the desk with all your schoolbooks
Set your clocks to ring at five.

Shopkeeper, leave your chalk,
   Housewife, your mending.
Look to your feather bed:
   'Morgen ist auch ein tag'

Ten o'clock.
Ten o'clock
No more interruptions.
Keys turned? Bolts drawn?
That was the third call.

Cl-o-ose your Bible, Dad.
Housewife, put your bonnet on.
Hus-band, your nightcap.
'Morgen ist…'

     All asleep.
That's the Hameliners!

From Chapter 2

Dreams

In all other cities,
   in mine, for instance, (out of bounds)
husbands see mermaids, and
   wives dream of Byrons.

Children see devils,
     and servants see horsemen.
But what can these, Morpheus,
     citizens so sinless

dream of at night – Say *what?*
     They don't need to think hard.
The husband sees – his wife!
     The wife sees her husband!

The baby sees a teat.
     And that beauty, fat of cheek,
sees a sock of her father's
     that she's been darning.

The Cook tries the food out.
     The 'Ober' gives his orders.
It's all as it ought to be,
     all as it ought to be.

As stitches go smoothly
     along a knitting needle
Peter sees Paul (what else?).
     And Paul sees Peter.

A grandfather dreams of
     grandchildren.
Journalists – of some full-stop!
     The maid – a kind master.

Commandments for Kaspar.
     A sermon for the Pastor.
To sleep has its uses,
     it isn't really wasteful!

The sausage-maker dreams of
     poods of fat sausages;
a judge of a pair of scales
     (like the apothecary).

Teachers dream of canes.
     A tailor of goods for sale.
And a dog of his bone?
     Wrong! He sees his collar!

The Cook sees a plucked bird.
   The laundress sees velveteen.
Just as it's been laid down
   in the prescription.

And what of the Burgomeister?
   Sleep is like waking
once you are Burgomeister
   what else can you dream about?

Except looking over
   the citizens who serve you.
That's what the Burgomeister
   sees: all his servants!

That's how things have to be!
   That's how they are arranged!
That's the prescription!
   That's the prescription!

(My tone may be playful – yes,
   the old has some virtue)
So let us not use up
   our rhymes over nothing.

As the Burgomeister sleeps, let's
   slip into his room (Tsar
of Works and Constructions!)
   How solidly the building stands …

It's worth our attention.

From *The Children's Paradise*

To live means – ageing,
turning grey relentlessly.
To live is – for those you hate!
Life has no eternal things.

In my kingdom: no butchers, no jails.
    Only ice there! Only blue there!
Under the roof of shivering waters
    pearls the size of walnuts

girls wear and boys hunt.
There's – a bath – for everyone.

Pearls are a wondrous illness.
Fall asleep then. Sleep. And vanish.

Dry twigs are grey. Do you want
scarlet? – Try my coral branch!

In my kingdom: no mumps; no measles,
    medieval history, serious matters,
no execution of Jan Hus. No discrimination.
    No more need for childish terrors.

Only blue. And lovely Summer.
Time – for all things – without measure.

Softly, softly, children. You're
going to a quiet school – under the water.

Run with your rosy cheeks
into the eternal streams.

Someone: Chalk. Someone: Slime.
Someone calling: Got my feet wet.

Someone: Surge. Someone: Rumble.
Someone: Got a gulp of lake!

2

Diving boys and swimming girls
Look, the water's on their fingers.

Pearls are scattered for them!
The water's at their ankles,

sneaking up their little knees. They cry:
– Chrys – o – lite.

Red moss! Blue caves!
(Feet go deeper. Skies rise higher.)

Mirror boxes. Crystal halls. Something's
been left behind, something grows closer

You're stuck up to the knees! Careful.
– Ah this chrys-o-prase!

The water is shoulder high on
little mice in schoolday clothes.

Little snub-nose, – higher, higher
now the water's at your throat.

It's sweeter than bed linen ...
– Crystals! Crystals!

In my kingdom: (The flute sounds the gentlest *dolce)*
    Time dwindles, eyes grow larger.
Is that a sea gull? or is it a baby's bonnet?
    Legs grow heavy, hearts grow lighter.

Water reaches to the chin.
Mourn, friends and relatives!

Isn't this a fine palace
for the burgomeister's daughter?

Here are eternal dreams, woods without pathways.
    The flute grows sweeter, hearts more quiet.
Follow without thinking. Listen. No need for thought!
    The flute becomes sweeter still, hearts even quieter.

– *Mutter.* Don't call me in for supper ...
                      Bu-u-bbles!

                                        1925

From *Poems to a Son*

Forget us, children. Our conscience
   need not belong to you.
You can be free to write the tale
   of your own days and passions.

Here in this family album
   lies the salt family of Lot.
It is for you to reckon up
   the many claims on Sodom.

You didn't fight your brothers
   my curly headed boy!
So this is your time, this is your day.
   The land is purely yours.

Sin, cross, quarrel, anger,
   these are ours. There have been
too many funerals held by now
   for an Eden you've never seen

whose fruit you never tasted.
   So now, put off your mourning.
Understand: they are blind
   who lead you, but then

our quarrel is not your quarrel,
   So as you rush from Meudon
and race to the Kuban
   children, prepare for battle

in the field of your own days.

January 1932

Homesickness

Homesickness! that long
exposed weariness!
It's all the same to me now
where I am   altogether lonely

or what stones I wander over
home with a shopping bag to
a house that is no more mine
than a hospital or a barracks.

It's all the same to me, captive
lion   what faces I move through
bristling, or what human crowd will
cast me out   as it must

into myself, into my separate internal
world, a Kamchatka bear without ice.
Where I fail to fit in (and I'm not trying) or
where I'm humiliated   it's all the same.

And I won't be seduced by the thought of
my native language, its milky call.
How can it matter   in what tongue I
am misunderstood by whoever I meet

(or by what readers, swallowing
newsprint, squeezing for gossip?)
They all belong to the twentieth
century, and   I am before time,

stunned, like a log left
behind from an avenue of trees.
People are all the same to me, everything
is the same, and it may be the most

indifferent of all   are these
signs and tokens which once were
native   but the dates have been
rubbed out: the soul was born somewhere.

For my country has taken so little care
of me that even the sharpest spy could
go over my whole spirit and would
detect no native stain there.

Houses are alien, churches are empty
everything   is the same:
But if by the side of the path one
particular bush rises
                              the rowanberry ...

                                                    1934

I opened my veins

I opened my veins.   Unstoppably
life spurts out with no remedy.
Now I set out bowls and plates.
Every bowl will be shallow.
Every plate will be small.
            And overflowing their rims,
into the black earth, to nourish
the rushes unstoppably
without cure, gushes
poetry ...

                                                    1934

Epitaph

1

Just going out for a minute –
left your work (which the idle
call chaos) behind on the table.
And left the chair behind when   you went where?

I ask around all Paris, for it's
only in stories or pictures
that people rise to the skies:
where is your soul gone, where?

In the cupboard, two-doored like a shrine,
look   all your books are in place.
In each line the letters are there.
Where has it gone to, your face?

Your face
your warmth
your shoulder

where did they go?

2

Useless with eyes   like nails to
penetrate the black soil.
As true   as a nail in the mind
you are not here, not here.

It's useless   turning my eyes
and fumbling round the whole sky.
Rain. Pails of rain-water. But
you are not there, not there.

Neither one of the two. Bone is
too much bone. And spirit is too much spirit.
Where is the real you? All of you?
Too much here. Too much there.

And I won't exchange you for sand
and steam. You took me for kin,
and I won't give you up for a corpse
and a ghost: a here, and a there.

It's not you, not you, not you,
however much priests intone
that death and life are one:
God's too much God, worm – too much worm!

You are one thing, corpse and spirit.
We won't give you up for the smoke of
censers
or flowers
on graves

If you *are* anywhere, it's here in
us: and we honour best all those who
have gone by despising division.
It is all of you   that has gone.

3

Because once when you were young and bold
you did not leave me to rot alive among
bodies without souls or fall dead among walls
I will not let you   die altogether.

Because, fresh and clean, you took me
out by the hand, to freedom   and brought spring leaves
in bundles into my house   I shall not
let you be grown over with weeds and forgotten.

And because you met the status of my
first grey hairs like a son   with pride
greeting their terror with a child's joy:
I shall not let you go grey into men's hearts.

4

The blow   muffled through years of
    forgetting, of not knowing:
That blow reaches me now like the song of a
    woman, or like horses neighing.

Through an inert building, a song of passion and
    the blow comes:
dulled by forgetfulness, by not knowing which is
    a soundless thicket.

It is the sin of memory, which has no eyes or
    lips or flesh or nose,
the silt of all the days and nights
    we have been without each other

the blow is muffled with moss and waterweed:
    so ivy devours the
core of the living thing it is ruining
    – a knife through a feather bed.

Window wadding, our ears are plugged with it
    and with that other wool
outside windows of snow and the weight of spiritless
    years: and the blow is muffled.

1935

Readers of Newspapers

It crawls, the underground snake,
crawls, with its load of people.
And each one   has his
newspaper, his skin
disease; a twitch of chewing;
newspaper *caries*.
Masticators of gum,
readers of newspapers.

And who are the readers? old men? athletes?
soldiers? No face, no features,
no age. Skeletons – there's no
face, only the newspaper page.

All Paris   is dressed
this way from forehead to navel.
Give it up, girl, or
you'll give birth to
a reader of newspapers.

Sway   he lived with his sister.
Swaying   he killed his father.
They blow themselves up with pettiness
as if they were swaying with drink.

For such gentlemen   what
is the sunset or the sunrise?
They swallow emptiness,
these readers of newspapers.

For news   read: calumnies.
For news   read: embezzling,
in every column   slander
every paragraph some   disgusting thing.

With what, at the Last Judgement
will you come before the light?
Grabbers of small moments,
readers of newspapers.

Gone! lost! vanished! so,
the old maternal terror.
But mother, the Gutenberg Press
is more terrible than Schwarz' powder.

It's better to go to a graveyard
than into the prurient
sickbay of scab-scratchers,
these readers of newspapers.

And who is it rots our sons
now in the prime of their life?
Those corrupters of blood
the *writers* of newspapers.

Look, friends   much
stronger than in these lines, do
I think this, when with
a manuscript in my hand

I stand before the face
there is no   emptier place
than before the absent
face of an editor of news-
                    papers' evil filth.

1935

Desk

1

My desk, most loyal friend
    thank you. You've been with me on
every road I've taken.
    My scar and my protection.

My loaded writing mule.
    Your tough legs have endured
the weight of all my dreams, and
    burdens of piled-up thoughts.

Thank you   for toughening me.
    No worldly joy could pass
your severe looking-glass
    you blocked the first temptation,

and every base desire
    your heavy oak outweighed
lions of hate, elephants
    of spite   you intercepted.

Thank you for growing with me
    as my need grew in size
I've been laid out across you
    so many years   alive

while you've grown broad and wide
    and overcome me.   Yes,
however my mouth opens
    you stretch out   limitless.

You've nailed me to your wood.
    I'm glad.   To be pursued.
And torn up.   At first light.
    To be caught.   And commanded:

Fugitive. Back to your chair!
    I'm glad you've guarded me
and bent my life away
    from blessings that don't last,

as wizards guide sleep walkers!
    My battles burn as signs.
You even use my blood to set out
    all my acts in lines —

in columns, as you are a pillar
    of light. My source of power!
You lead me as the Hebrews once
    were led forward by fire.

Take blessings now from me,
    as one put to the test, on
elbows, forehead, knotted knees,
    your knife edge   to my breast.

2

I celebrate thirty years
    of union   truer than love
I know every notch in your wood.
    You know the lines in my face.

Haven't you written them there?
    devouring reams of paper
denying me any tomorrow
    teaching me only today.

You've thrown my important letters
        and money   in floods together,
repeating: for every single verse
        today has to be the deadline.

You've warned me of retribution
        not to be measured in spoonfulls.
And when   my body will be laid out,
        great fool! Let it be on you then.

3

The rest of you can eat me up
        I just record your behaviour!
For you they'll find dining tables
        to lay you out.   This desk for me!

Because I've been happy with little
        there are foods I've never tasted.
The rest of you dine slowly.
        You've eaten too much and too often.

Places are already chosen
        long before birth for everyone.
The place of adventure is settled,
        and the places of gratification.

Truffles for you not pencils.
        Pickles instead of dactyls
and you express your pleasure
        in belches and not in verses.

At your head funeral candles
        must be thick-legged asparagus:
surely your road from this world
        will cross a dessert table!

Let's puff Havana tobacco
        on either side of you then;
and let your shrouds be made
        from the finest of Dutch linen.

And so as not to waste such
    fine cloth let them shake you
with left-overs and crumbs
    into the grave that waits for you.

Your souls at the   post mortem
    will be like stuffed capons.
But I shall be there naked
    with only two wings for cover.

1933–5

Bus

The bus jumped, like a brazen
evil spirit,   a demon
cutting across the traffic
in streets as cramped as footnotes,
it rushed on its way   shaking
like a concert-hall vibrating
with applause.   And we shook in it!
Demons too.   Have you seen
seeds under a tap? We were
like peas in boiling soup,
or Easter toys dancing in
alcohol.   Mortared grain!
Teeth in a chilled mouth.

What   has been shaken out   someone
could use for a chandelier:
all the beads   and the bones
of an old woman. A necklace
on that girl's breast. Bouncing.
The child at his mother's nipple.
Shaken without reference
like pears   all of us   shaken
in *vibrato,* like violins.
The violence shook our souls
into laughter, and back into childhood.

Young again. Yes. The joy of that
being thrown into girlhood! Or
perhaps further back, to become
a tomboy with toothy grin.
　　　It was as if the piper
　　　had lead us, not out of town, but
　　　right out of the calendar.

Laughter exhausted us all.
I was too weak to stand.
Enfeebled, I kept on my feet only
by holding your belt in my hand.

Askew, head on, the bus was
crazed like a bull, it leapt
as if at a red cloth,
to rush round a sharp bend
and then, quite suddenly
stopped.
　　　　　... So, between hills, the creature
　　　　　lay obedient and still.
　　　　　Lord, what blue surrounded us,
　　　　　how everywhere was green!

The hurt of living gone,
like January's tin.
Green was everywhere,
a strange and tender green.

A moist, uneasy noise of green
flowed through our veins' gutters.
Green struck my head open,
and freed me from all thinking!

A moist, wood-twig smoke of green
flowed through our veins' gutters.
Green struck my head open.
It overflowed me completely!

Inside me, warmth and birdsong.
You could drink both of them from
the two halves of my skull –
(Slavs did that with enemies).

Green rose, green shoots, green
fused to a single emerald.
The green smell of the earth had
struck deeply. (No buffalo feels that.)

Malachite. Sapphire. Unneeded.
The eye and ear restored –
Falcons don't see tillage,
prisoners don't hear birds.

My eye is ripe with green.
Now I see no misfortune
(or madness – it was true reason!)
to leave a throne and fall

on all fours like a beast
and dig his nose in the grass …
He wasn't mad, that sovereign
Nebuchadnezzar, munching

stalks of grass – but a Tsar,
an herbivorous, cereal-loving
brother of Jean-Jacques Rousseau …
This green of the earth has given
my legs the power to run

into heaven.
I've taken in so much
green juice and energy I am
as powerful as a hero.
The green of the earth has struck
my cheeks. And there it glows.

For an hour, under cherry trees,
God allowed me to think
that my own, my old, face
could be the same colour as these.

Young people may laugh. Perhaps
I'd be better off standing under
some old tower, than mistaking
that cherry-tree colour
for the colour of my

face …

With grey hair like mine? But then,
apple blossom is grey. And God has brought me close
to everyone of his creatures
I am *closer*   as well as *lower* …

a sister to all creation
from the buttercup to the mare –
So I blew in my hands, like a trumpet.
I even dared to leap!

As old people rejoice
without shame on a roundabout,
I believed my hair was brown
again, no grey streak in it.

So, with my branch of green
I could drive my friend like a goose,
and watch his sail-cloth suit
turn into true sails –

Surely my soul was prepared
to sail beyond the ocean.
(The earth had been a seabed –
it laughed now with vegetation.)

My companion was only slender
    in the waist.   His heart was thick.
(How his white canvas puckered,
    and came to rest in the green.)

Faith. Aurora. Soul's blue.
    Never dilute or measured.
Idiot soul!   And yet Peru
    will yield to the madness of it!

My friend became heavy to lead,
    as a child does for no reason,
(I found my own bold web
    as lovely as any spider's)

Suddenly   like a vast frame
for a living miracle: Gates!
Between their marble, I could
stand, like an ancient sign,

uniting myself and the landscape;
a frame in which I remain,
between gates that lead to no castle,
gates that lead to no farmhouse,

gates   like a lion's jaws
which let in light. Gates
leading to where? Into
happiness   came the answer,

twofold ...

Happiness? Far away.   North of here.
Somewhere else. Some other time.
Happiness? Even the scent is cold.
I looked for it once, on all fours.

When I was four years old, looking
for a clover with four leaves.
What do these numbers matter?
Happiness? Cows feed on it.

The young are in ruminant company
of two jaws and four hooves.
Happiness stamps its feet.
It doesn't stand looking at gates.

> The wood block and the well.
> Remember that old tale?
> Of cold water streaming past
> an open, longing mouth,
>
> and the water missing the mouth
> as if in a strange dream.
> There's never enough water,
> (the sea's not enough for me).

From opened veins, water
flows on to moist earth –
Water keeps passing by
as life does, in a dream.

And now I've wiped my cheeks
I know the exact force
of the streams that miss my hands
and pass my thirsting

mouth

> The tree, in its cloud of blossom,
> was a dream avalanche over us.
> With a smile, my companion compared it
> to a 'cauliflower in white sauce'.

> That phrase struck into my heart, loud
> as thunder. Now grant me encounters
> with thieves and pillagers, Lord, rather
> than bed in the hay with a *gourmand!*

A thief can rob – and not touch your face.
You'll be fleeced, but your soul will escape.
But a *gourmand* must finger and pinch, before
he puts you aside, to eat later.

I can throw off my rings. Or my fingers.
You can strip my hide, and wear it.
But a *gourmand* demands the brain and heart
to the last groan of their torment.

The thief will go off. In his pockets
my jewels, the cross from my breast.
A toothbrush ends all romance
with *gourmands.*
                    Don't fall in their hands!

And you, who could be loved royally
as an evergreen, shall be
as nameless as cauliflower in my mouth:
I take this revenge – for the tree!

                                        1934–6

When I look at the flight of the leaves

When I look at the flight of the leaves in
    their floating down on to the paving of cobbles
and see them swept up as if by an
    artist who has finished his picture at last

I think how (already nobody likes either
    the way I stand, or my thoughtful face)
a manifestly yellow, decidedly
    rusty leaf – has been left behind on the tree.

1936

From *Poems to Czechoslovakia*

6

They took   quickly, they took   hugely,
    took the mountains and their entrails.
They took our coal, and took our steel
    from us, lead they took also and crystal.

They took the sugar, and they took the clover
    they took the North and took the West.
They took the hive, and took the haystack
    they took the South from us, and took the East.

Vary   they took and Tatras   they took,
    they took the near at hand and far away.
But   worse than taking paradise on earth from us
    they won the battle for our native land.

Bullets they took from us, they took our rifles
    minerals they took, and comrades too.
But while our mouths have spittle in them
    the whole country   is still armed.

8

What tears in eyes now
weeping with anger and love
Czechoslovakia's tears
Spain in its own blood

and what a black mountain
has blocked the world   from the light.
It's time – It's time – It's time
to give back to God   his ticket.

I refuse to be. In
the madhouse of the inhuman
I refuse   to live.
With the wolves of the market place

I refuse   to howl.
Among the sharks of the plain
I refuse to swim   down
where moving backs make a current.

I have no need of holes
for ears, nor prophetic eyes:
to your mad world there is
one answer: to refuse!

1938

List of Collaborators

Literal versions of the poems by Marina Tsvetayeva were provided by the following:

Angela Livingstone

I know the truth
What is this gypsy passion for
  separation
We shall not escape Hell
We are keeping an eye on the girls
No one has taken anything away
You throw back your head
Where does this tenderness come
  from ?
Bent with worry
Today or tomorrow the snow will
  melt
Verses about Moscow
From Insomnia
Poems for Akhmatova
Poems for Blok
A kiss on the head
Praise to the Rich
The Poet
Poem of the End
Epitaph
Homesickness
Readers of Newspapers
When I look at the flight of the
  leaves
From Poems to Czechoslovakia

Daisy Cockburn

Verses
Anna

Valentina Coe

Poem of the Mountain

Simon Franklin

God help us   Smoke!

Ophelia: in Defence of the Queen
Wherever you are I can reach you
From Wires
Sahara
Appointment
Rails
You loved me
To Boris Pasternak
From The Ratcatcher. *From Chapter
  1 and from Chapter 2*
Desk
Bus

Vera Traill

From The Ratcatcher. *From
  'Children's Paradise'*

Jana Howlett

From Swans' Encampment

Bernard Comrie

Yesterday he still looked in my eyes

Maxwell Shorter

Some ancestor of mine
I'm glad your sickness
To Mayakovsky
It's not like waiting for post
My ear attends to you
As people listen intently
Strong doesn't mate with strong
In a world
I opened my veins

Cathy Porter

From Poems to a Son

MARGARITA ALIGER

Two lyrics from *For a Man on his Way*

I

I want to be your love
I want to be your strength
fresh wind
            daily bread
sky flying overhead

a path under your feet,
if you should lose your way
use it and don't look back;
if you grow tired and thirsty
look, I become a stream:
come close, bend down, and drink.

If you should want to rest
some night in the darkness
of mountainside or forest,
like smoke from a hut I'll rise
flare up   a flower of fire
you'll recognise me there.

I will gladly turn myself into
whatever you love in the world;
at dawn, look out of your window,
I'll be in whatever you see.

I will turn into a bird
(an iridescent tom-tit)
singing   at the day's end.
Yes, you must notice me,

there in the turning notes
of the nightingale
            in the leaves.

Can you see dew in those petals?
It is I.
                And the cloud
hanging above the garden.   Happy?
Then somewhere nearby
my love protects you.

I recognised you among many.
Now our paths are joined.
Do you understand, my love?
Wherever you are you will meet me.
You cannot help but see me.
You'll have to love me for ever!

VI

I do not want to meet you in the winter.
    You will always live in my soul as you were
in the springtime, with an uncovered head on
    that happiest day of my life, as in a dream.

I do not want to meet you in the winter.
    I am afraid of finding you older and drier,
of hearing you quarrel with your wife
    and seeing your indifference to a friend;

I'm afraid to discover that you can be
    bored, even for a moment, or finding out
you turn your collar up, like anyone else
    hurrying along under rainy clouds.

I want to remember you forever
    as my friend, my travelling companion,
loving mountains and cities, roads and rivers
    insatiably, always carefree, wonderstruck.

So, live like that. As I remember you,
    a man of impulses and nervous tension,
go on loving animals and trees.
    Know much, but go on asking many questions.

Look far ahead now in the distance
    with your transparent, wandering eyes.
Sometimes I feel at ease only to remember
    whatever else, that you are still alive.

So, while the day lasts, while the rivers flow
    rushing by in froth, I dream of
keeping you   exactly as you were then,
    how you were and how I'll always love you.

And even if I have invented you
    (a man that I should most desire to meet)
I do not want to have the fiction shattered.
    I do not want to meet you in the winter.

Great Expectations

The flame of kerosene flickers.
    Alone in the house with Dickens:
in the darkness around us burn
    fires of *Great Expectations*.

O how deeply he longed for
    happiness, poor young Pip!
This house without noise
    is filled with the gloom of war.

Is it so long since voices
    brightened the home with sound?
Pain has not blinded me.
    I can see the distant sails.

and feel the golden freedom,
    not yet throttled by sadness.
… It is the end of forty one.
    The Nazis close on Moscow.

The nearby battle booms
    (all expectations rising)
in Petrichshevskaya square
    Zoya goes to her death.

We cannot save her from torture,
   give her some water or help.
The guns blaze all around us.
   The night of siege is hollow.

Alarming the outline of buildings:
   no chink of light shows there:
the only ray that warms us
   is the light of great expectations.

My bitter love, where are you?
   Come back into my verse!
I'm already losing the marks
   of the threads that you tore loose.

Only the memory of early days
   brightens this cruel end,
that summer flash of expectation
   when we trembled like captives together.

Whatever comes upon us,
   whatever the days bring,
I remember poor young Pip
   and those fires of *Great Expectations!*

With everything changed, inside out;
   everything hurtful and bitter,
with the flight of great expectations
   something still strains forward.

Bad times are strangely similar
   whenever they strike home.
It is the end of forty one.
   The Nazis close on Moscow.

At the time of sharpest pain
   some star of great expectations
familiar from our childhood
   always appears for everyone

and the path towards it looks
   comforting however steep.
Perhaps even great achievements
   pale beside   great expectations!

'My lips are salt'

My lips are salt, and my eyelashes.
   I have forgotten nothing:
no grief, no happiness is lost
   of all that has happened to us.

There were no lies, no lies,
   no treachery or dishonour!
Along a path through rye
   near Moscow we walked together,

in a small field of bluebells
   we once sat on the grass;
from the steep bank of a hill,
   we watched carp in the river.

Centuries-old oaks bearing
   extremes of heat and snow
all know the story of our fate
   and tell it to one another.

Above the River Moskva
   you cannot guess the distance
or measure all the earth we walked
   once on those hills together.

And when we part for the last time
   (that is, when life is over),
the sound of our feet and hearts
   will still be heard by people

who may inherit all our
   light-blue earth, and sunset glow
this morning wind across the fields,
   and apple-blossom snow!

As we loved one another there
   let them love   whoever they are!

Two

Once again they've quarrelled on a tram,
  shamelessly indifferent to strangers.
I can't hide how much I envy them.
  I can't take my eyes off their behaviour.

They don't even know their good fortune,
  and not knowing is a part of their luck.
Think of it. They are together. Alive.
  And have the time to sort things out and make up.

To the Portrait of Lermontov

My twenty-six year old ensign,
please forgive me, please forgive
the twice as many years I've lived
in this bright world, where I still am.
Forgive me, please forgive me, for
every feast and every day, it's
been my fortune to have more,

twice as many more than you!
And yet if I've had twice your days
there has been room in them for twice
as many fears and injuries.
Who knows which century it was
easier to bear? Between us
who was luckier? What weighs more,
heavy blows the living feel, or
grass that's growing overhead?

You don't answer since you're dead.
And I won't answer. I'm alive ...

'If everything'

If everything I cannot learn to bear
   could only be turned into a
song or a story with a firm line
   the weight of grief would leave my heart at once,

as other people, men or women, share
   my pain, and help me to live through it.
This is why I first became a poet.
   I can't think of any other reason.

House in Meudon

Grey and dingy house in Meudon,
dull and grey old house in Meudon,
flat as board   four storeys high
uncoloured brick, unlit, unchosen
there by someone else's garage, like
a burnt-out candle, dripping wax:
there it was you lived, Marina.

Grey and dingy house in Meudon.
Nothing grows on that verandah.
There's no smile behind the window,
just a dead house, stiff with cold, with
no dogs, no cats and alone
deserted like a bivouac.

How long since the Russian language
was used there? To cry or laugh or
hide your misery from children,
suffer in,   or breathe, or be
written in notebooks until morning.
Now this upright narrow house
has fallen into French silence
with its gates closed at the bend.
It conjures up by day and night
all your memories in my heart.

From now on, to move or not, will
alter nothing. Magic cannot
change the bends that wait for you
hollows ahead, and more mirages –
houses by other people's garages.

Now I have it on my palm,
in my own hands: the dingy house.
Look, how bare it is, how lonely,
always facing down the road
three hundred metres. To the station.

– I must pack my bundle now.
– What's the hurry? Off to Paris?
What's the fever? What's the panic?
You've seen Berlin once already.
Do you want to go to Prague?
– No. I'd rather die. I'll go to
no more foreign cities. Ever.

I must go back to Trekhprudny,
to Granatny, Plyushikha, the Arbat …
Yes, let's be going. Soon, as soon
as can be. Fast. At a run.
Still the dingy house in Meudon –
Stubbornly, its black stare follows.
While you find your last dark river
Kama, rocks, insects, and that
small town that reaches down the hill.

To the Kama, then, from Meudon.
To be without a home or foothold.
Not to prison. Not to freedom.
With a great stone in your throat.
Two years. No address. No shelter.
Without a word. Without a word.
Without daughter. Without husband.
Only horror, hard frost, sirens,
and the war shriek overhead.

Still your son was with you, in that
wooden hut above the river.
Who was guilty then? Of what?
In that dark house, on that rough road.

All around you, Russia, Russia
danced in golden rings barefoot
in the small woods
                    on the steep banks,
Russia who had brought you up
a daughter once – then let you go.
So, did you displease her? How?
Because you went away from home
and lost yourself in foreign lands?
That she forgave you long ago.
Russia had not time, not then,
to understand you, all her women
wept in all the villages,
wagons always on the move
steppes on fire, and all her people
running away. How could she then
remember you? Or bother with you?
There you were. Behind the fence.
Yelabuga. The edge of war.
For no fault of yours forgotten.
Mother Russia. Mother Rus'.
This cold. Bleak. I am afraid.

What comes next Lord? Every August
is the end of summer. So
what happens? Every year
rains come and the hardest clay
erodes and crumbles. Winter comes.
Marina. How will you live through it?
The Kama will not move. No way
to cross. By foot or horse. No path
Or road. Only the snow. Blizzard.
No friend. Not even an enemy.
Only snow and snow and snow
like our landlady's featherbed!
You won't be able to leave the yard.
Marina. How will you live through it?
Even you can't handle this.
You've gone too far.
– Yes. This is it.
                    And your last trick?
                           A hempen rope.

For Neruda

Massive, heavy, with a small Kepi
   on his large head, dressed in
a well-cut suit, (well-made at least
   to make its owner comfortable)
so he is massive, heavy, strong,
   an undisturbed man and reliable,
who lives wherever he is as if
   in every cell of his body, every minute,
he thinks, acts, walks and breathes like
   a sailor or a miner or a lumberjack
or perhaps an aristocrat.
   What he most resembles
is a stone, from his native shore, a stone
   that has rolled down from the Cordillera
on the line between sea and sand;
   a stone, which time and wind and
the great ocean waves have given
   an intricate form   which is improbable
at heart   and yet altogether human.

'Much too happy'

Much too happy always
in the strength of your love
I see now, much too late,
that after all I was stronger.
I had the strength to bear it
all,   for as long as needed.
When you were most cruel
you were really begging for help.
Everything could have been saved
if I had taken it on!
And there's no one to say 'forgive me'
to now   since you are gone.
The powerless words burn
my lips. What's the use?
              And why
do people still declare
that I am left alive!

YUNNA MORITZ

Midday in Gantiadi

His eyelids are dark as coffee, the Southerner,
who has taken pancakes stuffed with lamb from
the hot meat dish in the cauldron,
and the sexual charm in his smile is
as calm as the life of a vegetable
or the brown flesh of Greek olives.

He draws me secretly towards him, as if
by oil of camphor-wood, or some
insidious attraction without name,
older than the power of any reptile
and more abrupt than a pirate attack,
as if he was marked out in metal for me.

It is wrong to evade what you know,
as black ravens do if their path
should happen to cross the path of a bat;
forget your finicky pretence
of working miracles, though you long for them,
and always go to sleep in their light,

because you will wake again in idleness
and not be morally outraged, your spirit has
already been initiated.
Drink the Muscatel, gulp down
its fragrance from your chipped cylinder.
And for your sin? – hope only for forgiveness!

'In twilight'

In twilight, in smells of whitewash,
    of housepaint, and of lime,
we drink a sparkling tropical tea
    beneath wet-wood scaffolding.

The painters and the carpenters
    have gone at least until morning;
on one elbow in an armchair
    Autumn drinks tea with us, leaning.

To put a house in repair
    is a test of heart and wit,
a frame of mind that brings back
    an image of hospital life.

A freezing sadness, sterile as
    a long needle enters my breast,
my soul feels the very pain of
    flesh drawn in by a thread!

It takes a jerk to return to
    courage and commonsense,
and to numb that part of me
    which responds yet remains unquenchable.

But so it is, in Florence,
    a piano begins to play for us
marvellous threepart inventions
    of Johann Sebastian Bach.

In Memory of François Rabelais

To lie at the edge of the forest
with your face in the earth is miraculous
for idleness is tender, and
can be possessed entirely
in vegetable joy just as
bees sing into clover.

Feel the space under the planet.
Hold on to grass and beetles.
Gulp down the smell of the zoo
on your own skin. We live among
fair booths, where time is short,
packed in together densely.

In paradise no more idols!
People do what they like
joyfully, bathing and lazing,
without any thought of manners.
The healthy spirit of Rabelais
rules the whole population there.

No better world to wait for!
Laughter rises easily
and stories. Pierrot can
dance on his drum as naked
as if he were in a bath-house.
The show is for everyone.

When laughter beats in your ears,
your soul knows it's immortal.
The freedom is like a mouthful
of wine   a breathing space
a forgetting of this life's brevity.
The saddest truth can be funny.

Now go back to your anthill,
put coffee on the stove there.
Chew at your greens for supper.
Enjoy the simplest flavour,
and as you do so savour
the strangeness of carrying on!

Once you can shout and laugh
like a monkey at death and fate
and how men and women act –
the pause is wholly blessed.
A laugh is the outrageous; sign
that your soul remains alive.

Unhealthy fevers shake us
in this stern world. Tormented,
by chasing after success,
we may lose all we possess.
Even our souls may leak away
then, and only return to us
with Hell and horned beasts!

Three lyrics from *Poems for her Sick Mother*

I

Whiteness   the whiteness of these skies
heavily clamping down over our bodies;
when the time comes our souls will pass through you
only too easily. So here I am, Lord,
blocking my mother's entrance to paradise
ready to curse the light blue roof of it
however you harass me into the cracks
like a snake   I won't give her up to you yet
gnawing stones and howling where I sit.
I shall refuse to let my mother past.

II

Misfortune is as huge
and heavy as this cold
I'm half-dead. Without home.
Without a roof   or wing

Alone under bare skies.
A stump of birchwood chair
my table drowned by rain
abandoned, covered in snow.

My pages rustled through
by icy winds. Mother!
Snow-girl. Small bird.
Snow-girl. Don't touch the fire!
The bonfire. Lie quite still.
Like a water drop on sand
like a red tear on my cheek.
Don't touch! Lie quite still.

Don't touch the fire. Lie there.
Perhaps death will hold back.
And spring will come. Spring!
With peas and beans returning
a star will fall in the well
or a single drop of dew.
Spring birds where are you flying?
A frail old woman can so easily
dwindle away to nothing
before you return. It's hard not to!

I wait in the hospital courtyard
and sitting here make up my prayer.
Trees.   Trees.   Lake.   Lake.
While there is time to spare
before my mother's small body is bruised
yellow and blue. Please. Give me
a small piece of spring, whose
time will come anyway, spring always comes:
beans appear, peas come up,
and small prickly cucumbers.
I won't believe it, I won't believe it. No.

It is impossible mother should go
for ever   before the first strawberries.
And yet the stars are bright over the fields.
There is snow in the wind over the poplars.
Against the wall a snowdrift. Like a breast.
And we are children. Grant us a little spring!

V

A flight of birds has arrived in
their many-coloured coats.
In the yard, grass is thick
like fur on a baby bear –
on a green bear, yes, a green one,
the smallest and the youngest bear.
People are walking about,
and animals. Bless all walkers!
Look, the city will survive,
every village will survive.
For the sun will shine in
the light blue heights again.
The pear will come to fruit,
like potato, like wheat ...
And Mother is learning to walk.

Don't fall, don't fall, little tear,
it mustn't be slippery for her!

'Midnight cold'

Midnight cold of oxygen
bronze vitriol of stars:
spirals of scorching roses
are kindled around my window

and nobody moves along
the empty path in the distance
where I see a tall shadow,
too tall for any human.

I recognise the Muse.
Her steps sing every syllable.
At the sound, roses break loose
and float down to her feet.

Her wide stare is serious
her lips are full and firm.
Look how she moves right through
that splendid thought – a bush –

to be lit up by a storm
even as she walks the clouds
bearing a dark-red parcel
of roses in toil-worn hands.

Autumn Morning Frost

I wake up, cold and dark. In Moscow
the radiators are not yet heated. Boreas
blows in from outside the door, where
cats and dogs go numb with cold, and the wind
has long ago pulled out cereals and flowers
with its pincers from the fields and streets.
My hands freeze on the blanket.
My dawn thoughts form without tenderness
into clouds on a mountain, or
dark herds clutched in autumn boredom.
I am like some hero carefully hiding
the way his feelings have darkened with absence.
I observe every sound, every sign.
Above the tin-plate roofs, a sheet which
clattered all night like a stutterer,
now twined, makes the sound of a kiss.
I wake up. To decipher the habits
of the spirit in savage gloom.
I wake up. The sky in the east
is as dark as a boarded-up barn.
The troughs of crumbly gutters are
tormented by the shrieks and barks.
I know this place. It's Paradise.
Sit face to face. Run your fingers over
the strings of the Orphic lyre.
Breathe through the dullest lesson.
Domestic noises of laundry, tidying,
and chopping-up carry everywhere.

But a child, still flushed with play,
takes a woolly lamb in its hands
and walks along the damp street following
an upright shadow resembling
an arrow   in a great bow.
And the antique sciences whisper
both the bow and the lyre were imagined
by that boy once before in a dark time.
For the world is always one and dual. Another
dimension lives in the background of every sound!

'Now we'll go'

Now we'll go homeward
     in search of a bed
in a silver pillar of
     Christmas snow

and there with one toe
     push the heel of the other
and so take our boots off
     without any bother:

then inside the coffee pot
     some strange drink rustles.
We are reminded
     how no soul is bounded;

and no talent can be
     a convenient mixture
of things that we like only:
     but what is best and what is worst.

'The bell'

The bell in the hollow chapel
and the bell in the throat of the donkey
fill me with love.   Such depths
their beauty opens to me.

Here southern valleys feed on
mad fruitfulness! Asian teahouse
noises rise in a garden of
persimmons, mandarins, *feikhoas*.

How easily work is rewarded with crops here!
Rather as the herds of those going straight to
the braziers and bonfires of hell multiply!
The world after death is another great enterprise!

New accounts for it open. Juice and fat
begin to flow. Sweet smoke goes up the chimney.
But we still want our freedom, and long to live
with nothing to darken our fate, don't we?

Even though the way our days are arranged has
been exposed to the bone, to the Hiroshima bomb.
We must hold on, keep going, you must understand,
without my love your world is unbearable.

BELLA AKHMADULINA

Music Lessons

Marina, how I love to know that
like everyone else, like me –
who cannot speak now through my frozen throat
because to speak of it is like swallowing ice –
to know that you, a creature of light! of snow!
were like the rest of us, given lessons in music.
And there was a waste of teaching, almost as if
to the sound of laughter and tears among
the gods, a candle had been given rules for glowing.
You and the piano, equally dark
creatures, could not get on together.
Two perfect circles, you touched each other's
foreign language, remotely as deaf mutes.
Sombrely you were drawn together in
that insoluble and hostile encounter:
a piano and you! Stubborn and silent,
the voice of music still weak in you both
Marina, defenceless child, that decided
the matter. What is a piano? It is only
silent and a prisoner until some
friend puts a finger on C sharp.
But you were alone. There was no help for you.
Your music had to be learnt with difficulty:
without troubling the source of your pain,
you had to open yourself to bleed in sound.
Marina, C! C! for childhood,
doh, your destiny! *Doh! Re!* if speech,
doh, for everything that comes afterwards!
As we both leant forward our foreheads in
that universal pose before the piano together,
like you! like you! I grasped the stool, that
merry-go-round of a worthless pedagogue,
to try unwinding the same equator
which has already torn away your beret
and now lies whistling around your head.

Marina, the intention of all this springs from
the beauty of uttering just once and perfectly, the cry:
I am like you! like you! I wanted to
shout that out with joy – but instead, I weep.

Fever

I must be ill, of course. I've been shivering
for three days now like a horse before the races.
Even the haughty man who lives on my landing
has said as much to me:
Bella, you're shaking!

Please control yourself, this strange disease of yours
is rocking the walls, it gets in everywhere.
My children are driven mad by it, and at night
it shatters all my cups and kitchenware.

I tried to answer him: Yes,
I do tremble,
more and more, though I mean no harm to anyone.
But tell everyone on the floor, in any case,
I've made up my mind to leave the house this evening.

However, I was then so jerked about by
fever, my words shook with it; my legs
wobbled; I couldn't even bring my
lips together into the shape of a smile.

My neighbour, leaning over the banister,
observed me with disgust he didn't hide.
Which I encouraged.
– This is just
a beginning. What happens next, I wonder.

Because this is no ordinary illness. I'm sorry to
tell you, there are as many wild and
alien creatures flashing about in me
as in a drop of water under a microscope.

My fever lashed me harder and harder, and
drove its sharp nails under my skin. It was
something like the rain whipping an
aspen tree, and damaging every leaf.

I thought: I seem to be moving about rapidly
as I stand here, at least my muscles are moving.
My body is out of my control completely.
The thing is freely doing whatever it likes.

And it's getting away from me. I wonder if
it will suddenly and dangerously disappear?
Like a ball slipping out of a child's hand,
or a piece of string unreeling from a finger?

I didn't like any of it. To
the doctor
I said, (though I'm timid with him)
— you know, I'm a proud woman! I can't have my
body disobeying me for ever!

My doctor explained:
Yours is a simple disease,
perhaps even harmless, unfortunately
you are vibrating so fast I can't examine you.

You see, when anything vibrates, as you are,
and its movements are so very quick and small,
the object is reduced, visibly speaking
to — nothing. All I can see is: mist.

So my doctor put his golden instrument
against my indefinite body, and a sharp
electric wave chilled me at once
as if I had been flooded with green fire

and the needle and the scales registered horror.
The mercury began to seethe with violence.
The glass shattered, everything splashed about,
and a few splinters drew blood from my fingers.

— Be careful, doctor, I cried. But
he wasn't worried.
Instead, he proclaimed: Your
poor organism is
now functioning normally.

Which made me sad. I knew myself to belong
to another norm than he had ever intended.
One that floated above my own spirit only
because I was too narrow for such immensity.

And those many figures of my ordeals had
trained my nervous system so that now
my nerves were bursting through my skin, like old
springs through a mattress, screeching at me.

My wrist was still out of shape with its huge
and buzzing pulse, that always had insisted
on racing greedily: Damn it then, run free, I cried
I'll choke with you, as Neva chokes St Petersburg.

For at night my brain has become so sharp with
waiting, my ear so open to silence, if
a door squeaks or a book drops, then –
with an explosion – it's the end of me.

I have never learnt to tame those beasts
inside, that guzzle human blood.
In my presence, draughts blow under doors!
Candles flare – before I extinguish them!

And one enormous tear is always ready
to spill over the rim of my eyes.
My own spirit distorts everything.
My own hell would corrupt heaven.

The doctor wrote me out a Latin scrip.
The sensible and healthy girl in
the chemists shop was able to read the
music in it from the punctuation.

And now my whole house has been softened by
the healing kiss of that valerian,
the medicine has licked into every
wound I have, with its minty tongue.

My neighbour is delighted, three times he
has congratulated me on my recovery,
(through his children). He has even
put in a word for me with the house management.

I have repaid a few visits and debts already,
answered some letters. I wander about
in some kind of profitable circles.
And no longer keep any wine in my cupboard.

Around me – not a sound, not a soul.
My table is dead, dust hides everything on it.
My blunt pencils like illiterate
snouts, are all lying in darkness.

And like a defeated horse, all my
steps are sluggish and hobbling now.
So all is well. But my nights are
disturbed with certain dangerous premonitions.

My doctor has not yet found me out. However
it will not long be possible to
fool him. He may have cured me once, but
soon I know I shall burn and freeze again.

A snail in its grave of bone I am
for the moment saved by blindness and silence –
but still the horns of sick antennae itch
and will rise up once again from my forehead.

Star-fall of full stops and hyphens, I
summon your shower to me! I want to
die with the silvery goose-flesh of
water nymphs burning in my spine.

Fever! I am your tambourine, strike me
without pity! I shall dance, like
a ballerina to your music, or
  live like a chilled puppy in your frost.

  So far I haven't even begun to
  shiver. No, let's not even discuss that. Yet
  my observant neighbour is already
  becoming rather cold to me when we meet.

I Swear

by that summer snapshot taken
on someone else's porch, skewed to one
side, that looks so like a gibbet, and
points a way out of the house not into it;
where you are wearing some violent sateen dress that
cramps the muscles of your throat like armour;
and are simply sitting there, with the endurance of a
tired horse after the labour of
singing out to the end all your grief and hunger.
I swear: by the photo, and your delicate pointed
elbows, which are as child-like as the smile of surprise
that death uses to lure children to itself and leaves
as mark upon their faces for evidence.
I swear: by the painful burden of remembering
how I gulped your airless grief from the
breathless rush of your lines, and had to
keep clearing my throat until it bled.
Yes, by your own presence, which I have stolen,
burgled, taken for myself, as if forgetting that
you belong to God, who cannot get enough of you;
and by that starved emaciation which
killed you at the end with its rat tooth.
I swear: by the blessed Motherland herself, even if
she grossly abandoned you like an orphan;
and your beloved African, that great genius of
kindness, whose own end was unkind, now
as a statue watching over small children.
By those children! And the Tversky Boulevard!
And your own sad rest in Paradise, where
there is neither trade nor torment for you!
I swear: to kill that Yelabuga, your
Yelabuga, so that our grandchildren
can sleep soundly. Old women may still frighten
them at nights, not knowing the power of her
'Sleep little child, quietly, quietly, for
blind Yelabuga is coming to catch you.'
And with all her tangle of legs truly she will
hasten towards me crawling with horrible speed.
But I shall bring my boot down on her
tentacles without saying any more, and

put my weight on my heel, and my toe-cap into
the back of her neck, and keep it there.
Then the green juice of her young will burn
the soles of my feet with their poison, but I'll
hurl the egg that ripens in her tail
into the earth, that bottomless earth!
And not say a word of the porch in the photograph.
I will not speak of Marina's homeless death.
I swear it. Even while in
the dark, and in the stench of silt,
with the toads in the well about her, she
has one yellow eye fixed in my direction:
The Yelabuga
swears her own oath – to kill me!

Winter

Winter, to me your gestures are
    cold and careful; yes, in
winter there is something
    gentle as medicine,

or why else would sickness
    put out trusting hands
into that season, from its own
    torture and darkness?

Weave your magic, then,
    my love, let the kiss
of one curl of ice
    brush over my forehead.

Soon I shall trust any
    deception, and look without fear
into the eyes of dogs, as I
    press close to the trees:

and forgive, playfully, with a
    run, turn and jump; and
after a bout of forgiveness
    forgive again,

become like a winter's day:
    empty and oval, though
in comparison to such
    presence, always small,

I shall turn to nothing, and
    so call over the wall,
not some shadow of myself, but light
    I shall not block at all.

Night

Now on three sides the darkness grows deeper
    with the coming of the dawn, and still my
hand has no courage to reach through the solid
    air to the white paper on the table.

For reason cannot honestly resist my
    sense of limitation! Now I cannot
let my hand write any of those careless
    phrases that once gave me joy.

In darkness there are always many meanings;
    it is easy to mistake the euphoria of
midnight, and a burning head that comes from
    slackness and caffeine – for sharp intelligence.

But evidently I have not damaged my
    brain altogether with my insane vigils.
I understand excitement is no merit,
    however hot; I do not think it talent.

It would be sinful to ignore that misery! Yet
    the temptation is sweet. How small and innocent
a gesture: to destroy the anonymity of night, and
    call all things within it by their right names.

Even as I try to keep my hand still
    each object flirts with me, and shows its
own beauty, I am invited with
    every movement now to render homage

to each thing, convinced of my love,
    whose small voice growls and begs
to have its soul celebrated in song –
    for which it needs my voice.

And I want to thank the candle, and to have
    its lovely light known everywhere, I would
offer tireless epithets as
    caresses. And yet I fall silent.

Under this torture of numbness, what pain –
    not to confess even with one word
the splendour of everything my love looks
    upon from darkness with stern eyes.

Why should I be ashamed? Aren't I free in
    an empty house, in a flood of snow, to
write, however poorly? at least to name
    the house, the snow, and the blue window?

A sheet of paper is defenceless. I pray
    God to keep me modest. Here I sit
before a clear and most ingenuous candle that
    lights my face now floating into sleep.

'For how many years'

For how many years along this street of mine have I
    overheard those footsteps – of my friends leaving.
And the darkness outside my window draws pleasure
    in witnessing every sluggish departure.

That is your stern character, Solitude, as
    you flash an iron compass; how coldly
now do you close your circle round me
    without attending to my useless protest.

Summon me, then, with some reward, since I
    have become your creature, and console myself
with your favours; let me rest against you
    and wash myself in the pale blue of your frost.

In your forest, on my toes, allow me to
    reach the slow peak of one strained gesture in
your foliage, and raise the leaves to my face
    so I may feel – to be desolate is a blessing.

Give me the quiet of your libraries,
    severe melodies in concert halls;
wise power – that is the way we forget
    those who are dead and those not yet alive.

So I shall learn wisdom and sadness together,
    and things will yield their hidden meanings up;
even Nature leaning on my shoulder
    may reveal her childish secrets to me.

But out of all the darkness, tears, and the
    forgetting of what is lost for ever,
the fine features of my friends will
    appear briefly to me, before dissolving.

Twelve lyrics from *Rain*

I

All morning I've had this Rain around me.
  Rudely, I kept on saying: Leave me alone!
So it drew back, but soon there it was again
  as sad and loving as a little daughter.

Rain. On my back. Stuck there like a wing.
  I reproached it: Here, you
  shameless, useless thing!
Think of the tears of some market gardener
  and water the flowers.
What do you find in me?

Meanwhile a heatwave was burning everywhere
  which the Rain ignored. And kept on until
there were children whirling all around me
  as if I were some kind of water-sprinkler.

Then I became crafty. Went in a café.
  Sat myself down at a quiet corner table.
But there was the Rain again. Through the glass.
  Motioning towards me, like a beggar.

So I went outside. And at once my face
  felt a wet slap. Immediately
(sorry and bold together) the Rain licked
  my lips, smelling warm as a wet puppy.

I must have looked stupid. As I
  tied a damp headscarf round my neck.
The Rain sat splayed on my shoulders like
  a monkey.
And the town was embarrassed by the whole thing.

While the Rain was delighted to find me helpless.
  It tickled my ear gently with a child's finger. And
all the while everywhere else dried out.
  Except me. I was soaked to the skin.

II

But I had an invitation to a house, where
    decorous people would be waiting for me,
a house with floors of amber water and
    a candelabra like a moon above them.

And I wondered: What shall I do with this Rain?
    It doesn't seem to intend to go away.
It will make a mess on the floor. And ruin the carpets.
    They won't even let me in if I bring it with me.

So I spoke to it firmly: Look, as you imagine
    I'm kind, but everything has a limit.
Absolutely: You can't come any further.
    At this the Rain looked up at me like an orphan.

— Damn you then. Come! I said:
    Though I don't understand what love holds us together.
A curse on this most peculiar weather!
    Forgiven, the Rain went skipping on ahead.

III

My host's invitation was something of
    an undeserved honour. However, I
appeared, dripping water like a beaver,
    and rang his bell at six o'clock precisely.

The Rain was hiding somewhere at my back.
Tickling as it sadly breathed down my neck.
Steps. Peephole. Pause. A lock turns.
I began to apologise: I've brought this Rain.

Do you think perhaps it could wait outside in the porch?
since it's much too wet, and too long anyway
to get into a room?
— What? said my astonished
host, and went white in the face.

IV

And I had loved that house, always, for
    the dance of lightness that was everywhere
and because elbows caught on no sharp corners
    there, and no knives slashed at people's fingers.

I loved it all. The slow rustle of
    the hostess' silk, and the scarf over her face,
And best of all, I loved that sleeping beauty
    captive in the sideboard: crystal glass,

    there, with the seven colours of the spectrum; it was
        lifeless and lovely in its transparent coffin.
    But I could not dream of that ... The ritual of
        greetings, began, formal as any opera.

V

To put it mildly, the mistress of that house would
    never have bothered to hide her dislike of me,
except for the fear of being thought old-fashioned.
    that restrained her, which was perhaps a pity.

– How *are* you? (And how could
    so haughty a slender throat hold back the thunder?)
– Thank you, I answered hastily: I feel
    like a sow that's been wallowing in the mud.

(I don't know what came over me. I meant
to say with some polite
gesture: I'm fine.
And much better for seeing you again.)

But she began to speak at once
You know, it's a disgrace, for someone like you, with so much talent
to walk so far. In all this rain!
Then everyone started to shout together.
– Bring her up to the fire! To the fire with her!

And once upon a time in another age
it could have happened to a beating drum
in the market place, with music perhaps and jeers
you would have cried:
To the fire, with her, to the fire!

— Hello then, and leap up at me, Fire!
    Brother, dog of many tongues, now lick
my hands m your great tenderness.
    For you are the Rain also. Your burn is wet!

— Your monologue is rather peculiar,
    my host said tartly.
— But never mind, blessings on green sheets!
    There's always charm in a new generation.

— Don't listen to me, I'm delirious, I said.
    It's all the fault of the Rain. All day it's
been pursuing me everywhere, like a devil.
    It's only the Rain that's getting me into trouble.

Then, suddenly, through the window I saw
    my faithful Rain, sitting alone and crying.
And two tears swam into my eyes, and they
    were the last traces of water left in me.

VI

Now, glass in hand, another woman guest, who
    looked as vague as a pigeon on a cornice,
asked me in a voice refined and waspish
    — Tell me, is it true your husband's rich?

— Is he? I don't know. Not specially.
    Yes, I suppose, work comes so easily
to him. But may I tell you a secret?
    There's something incurably poor in me.

And then my tongue ran away with me,
    — Did you know? I've taught him to cast
spells, on anything of value, so it turns
    into a circle of water, a weasel   or grass.

I'll show you how it's done. Give me your ring.
  We'll soon take that star out of its setting.
(But of course, she wouldn't let me have it
  and turned away from me like a stunned thing.)

— And I want you to know something else,
  I yelled after her, my tongue on fire.
(as though the rain still had control of me)
  — My deepest urge is to fall dead in the gutter.

VIII

Meanwhile to amuse the guests, some
  new family show was about to begin;
they were letting into the sitting room
a lace-clad silver cloud of children.

Hostess, please forgive me! I am evil.
  I've lied and behaved badly. Now I see
from your lips, like those of a glass blower
  a bottle of the purest glass appear,

a wholly-filled vessel of your spirit:
  your child, who is most delicately cast,
the outline of his body firm and even.
  I knew nothing, do not judge me harshly.

Your savage genius must be falling, hostess,
  into despair, day and night to be
forced to lower that monstrous head of his
  over this child, over this son of yours.

The Rain summoned my lips down to her hand
and I wept:
— Forgive me, please forgive,
your eyes are pure, and you must understand.

IX

Meanwhile the children struck up in chorus nearby

In times like these we have
    to have some kind of laugh.
Ha. Ha. There was a certain Jew
    and this Jew had a wife.

His wife would puff and blow
    and laboured hard and long
to make a little penny grow
    the size of a great house.

New little metal piece
    you ripen like a fruit
and rise up as the sun must rise
    to decorate the sky.

All this is just in play
    our turn and party trick.
What fun! And yet how grim to be
    brought up in this century.

We're only children now
    but grow up in our sleep
as little copper coins grow
    inside the treasury.

All our parental sins
    we have redeemed you'll find.
Vulgarity is not a sin,
    it brings a cosy mind.

From anger and from pain
    it proves our saviour:
and so we bend to kiss your
    velvet hem, great Queen.

X

Then laziness like an illness unfolded me
    and my arms moved strangely from my shoulders,
as I kept my glass warm in my hand like a bird
    and its open beak went peep-peep. Straight at her.

Hostess, have you ever felt remorse
    bending over your son, asleep in the morning
as you fed the milk of your poisoned breast
    into his greedy mouth that open wound?

Suppose that in him, as in an egg of pearl,
    slept a coiled spring of music
hidden like a rainbow in a white bud?
    Or like the muscle of beauty in a face?

As in Sashenko, slept unawakened Blok?
    You she-bear, to give yourself what pleasure
did you go hunting with your hungry teeth
    into your cub's fur to crack God like a flea?

XI

The hostess poured me out another cognac.
    – You're feverish. Warm yourself at the fire
Farewell, my Rain!
It is so sweet and so full of pleasure,
    to feel the tip of my tongue in this cold tingle.

How strangely this wine smells of roses.
Wine – I think only you are blameless.
The atom of the grape is split in me
and so begins the war of the two roses.

Spirit of wine, I am your delinquent
prince, tied between two bent trees.
Tear me apart! Without fear! One crack
and death will separate me from myself.

And now I am bigger and more tender.
Look – I am as kindly as a clown.
I am cast at your feet and bowing down
and already your doors and windows feel like cages.

Lord, what strange goodness, I feel now.
Hurry! While I weep here. On my knees.
I love you. Only a cripple's shyness
whitens my cheeks, and gives my lips their twist.

How can I serve you by one action?
Please hurt me, at least spare me no pain.
Here is my skin, stretched out with space for wounds, and
waiting as a canvas for paint.

I love you without measure, without shame.
And my embrace is round, as the sky itself.
We all share the same source. We are brothers.

Rain, my child. Come here, straightaway!

XII

Then a shiver ran down every spine
    and in quiet darkness the hostess screamed
as orange marks like rust suddenly
    appeared in streaks upon the white ceiling.

And down poured the Rain. They caught at it
    with tins, pushed it with brooms and brushes.
It escaped. And flew up in their cheeks
    or formed like liquid cataracts in their eyes.

It danced a strange and surprising can-can,
    and rang playfully on the restored crystal.
Then the house snapped its vicious jaws
    over it. Like a man-trap, tearing muscle.

The rain with a look of love and longing even as it
    soiled the floor, crawled to me on its belly;
even while men, lifting their trouser legs,
    kicked at it, or jabbed it with their heels.

They captured it with a floor-cloth and then
squeamishly wrung it out in the lavatory.
Until in a voice made suddenly hoarse and wretched
I shouted out
— Don't touch. It belongs to me.

It was alive, like a child or an animal.
Now may your children live in torment and misery.
Blind people, whose hands know nothing of mystery
why have you chosen to stain the Rain in blood?

The lady of the house whispered to me
— Remember,
you will have to answer for all this.
I burst out laughing:
I know what I shall answer!
You are disgusting. Now please let me pass.

XIII

I looked so wretched — passers by were alarmed
So I kept on saying
— Never mind. Forget it.
Even this episode will soon pass.
And on the parched asphalt
kissed the last drop of water.

For now the bare earth had become white hot,
and the sky-line around the city was pink.
The panic-stricken bureau of weather forecasts
made no promise of any other downpour.

'You were sleeping'

You were sleeping, today, while I was looking about us
into the shadows, a horseman on patrol.
It was then I understood exactly how late it was:
how death is waiting on stage, and how everything passes,
and though it looks innocent to scribble these lines
poetry is no longer private as prayer.
This generation demands performance. The guilt of that
I take on without the gift or desire for it.
For your sake I take on the shame of pretence
so that in me may be seen some hint of the past,
of how it might be with Marina and Anna alive
when poetry and conscience could live together.
So now in my throat, which is clean and clumsy,
an echo sounds of the ancient Russian word.
I have become an ambiguous, homely ghost
of two poets whose lives can never return.
I have inherited the tenderness that is theirs,
as much as I can bear, for more would murder me.
I understand how little I'm worth myself.
Yet, God knows, something links me to my listeners.
Perhaps the most virtuous thing would be silence itself,
which is the only certain way to keep lips from lying.
If that's impossible, then take away my voice
my last voice, and allow me to live honourably
until I leave everyone   whenever that may be!
At least my spirit is without cunning,
remains vigilant, and does not choose
the favours of this world, without fear of the next.
So I burn to speak truth, and I serve deceit
and must while I have life and energy.

YEVGENY YEVTUSHENKO

Poem

Do you think of her, geranium Yelabuga?
    That woman of the cities long ago
who smoked like other people cry, smoked
    all the time, your harsh, home-grown tobacco.

This is where, dead-tired, she had to go
    begging for linen to wash. So now
let me stand here, too, Marina;
    for a moment let me share your place.

An old woman, worn out with opening her
    wooden gate, said: I don't know why they
keep on coming; at my age it's torture.
    Well, I'd sell this house but who would buy it?

Yes, I remember the woman. Strict. I knew
    washing linen wasn't her job. She
never did learn how to roll her own fags, either
    so I had to do it for her. Not that rope though!

And yet that wretched hemp was
    kind to her; for the last time
she had the chance to wet her parched
    lips again with the frozen Kama.

But look at it – a nail! Not a hook. Clumsy.
    Used for the yokes of horses, too low to
reach for, still less hang from:
    it would have been as easy for her to choke!

And then that old woman, who had lived right
    through the famine, spoke to me with deference.
'And how can I get *rid* of this nail now?' she asked,
    touching it. 'Do you know what I should do?

Please, listen, be kind, and tell me one thing.
    How was it she came to kill herself?
You seem to have some kind of education, so
    perhaps you understand, and can help me.'

'Granny, this small room fills me with fear. All
    I really want is to fall on your shoulder and
cry with you. Remember: there is only
    murder in this world. Suicide has no existence here.'

NIKA TURBINA

'We speak a different language'

We speak a different language,
you and I.
The script may be the same,
but the words are strange.
You and I
live on different
islands, even though
we are in the same apartment.

1983

Long Distance Calls

Long distance calls
are in a race with God
all around the planet —
who can win it?
Your noise breaks through the glass
between the Lord and me.
I'm finished with such calls,
finished with calls!

I'll speak to Him in silence
(only our eyes meeting)
of how to save the earth
that is so sick of shouting.
And as the grass is rustled,
and leaves swirl in the wind
over my wounded earth,
we will speak in silence
of how not
to kill childhood.

1983

'Rain, night, a broken window'

Rain, night, a broken window
and shards of glass
stuck up in the air
like leaves the wind does not pick up.

Suddenly, there is a sound of ringing ...
That is exactly how
a human life breaks off.

1981

I Will Clean the House

I will clean the house
and put the furniture
in empty corners.
I will wash the floor
and fix the rugs,
and then sit down.
Behind the window panes
the rain will splash
and the day will punish me
with horrible loneliness.
I want so much
to go around the gate
and into the garden,
so I can look at all the flowers there.
But every morning instead
I start the day dusting,
and shutting the windows
against the wind.

1983

'Where are you living now'

Where are you living now
invisible soul?
Your tiny home
must be lovely.
You are wandering
alone in the city
invisible soul
and I can't see you.

1983

Remembrance

I want to sit alone with you
I want to sit alone
near the old house,
the house that stands
by the river of memory.
The print of your bare foot
smells of last summer's sun,
where you and I wandered
on the still unmown grass.
The skies were blue,
and disappeared beyond the outskirts.
Voices rang out
and that's all I remember.
The accounting of the days
has reached an end.
Like a flock of birds
all the days
have gathered at our feet.
I don't know what to feed them,
there are no lines left.

1981

Three Oranges

I'll bring home
three oranges in
a blue handkerchief.
There are city smells of
gas and cold,
and I blow on my fingers,
but suddenly
there are three oranges on the street
like a circle of sun.
Feet, wheels,
sledges in the slush ...
What I see are three oranges
burning in a blue handkerchief

and the sky and the garden.

1983

I Want Kindness

How often
I catch sidelong glances
and sharp words hurt me
like arrows
I implore you – listen! You must not
destroy the shortlived
childlike dreams in me.
My day is so small,
and I want kindness
so much
for everyone
even those
who aim
at me.

1983

'Sing me a lullaby, rock me'

Sing me a lullaby, rock me
to sleep, cover me with a blanket:
deceive me with your lulling,
give me your dreams in the morning.

On some days the image of
the sun is bluer than ice,
put that under my pillow
in the morning, but don't wait.

Listen, don't wait.
Childhood has run away from me.

1982

'As my lashes close, the day ends'

As my lashes close, the day ends
but I can't sleep.
I think about the passing day
which has gone by without
reaching the night,
about streets exhausted by people
and streetlights, weary
with the effort of shining
and about this house in which I can't sleep,
until sleep, an anxious grey bird,
flies up to me suddenly
at daybreak.
Now wake up, little thing,
early in the morning
and you'll see how
your streetlight has been resting,
laughter has filled the crossroads,
and a long time has gone by since evening.

1981

LOUIS RENÉ DES FORÊTS

From *The Shrews of the Sea*

Time to return, and my fever it is carries me to the
furthest edge of the shore-line to find some shelter;
slant as a hooked fish I am already moving now with
sea-weed on my head for a crown, on fire, I rush to
prick the red-brown fog of a late spring.
My feet rasp over that grating mosaic of the seas'
wreckage, there are knife-shells, blue as jays, dead starfish
and verminous excrement, potsherds with cutting edges, I am
no more than a beast that groans as it is taken,
and my throat is torn with an exhausting scream:
terror is sharp, and the wind also, yet
nothing diverts the pure line of my trajectory,
not deep pockets of squirting water, nor some bushy stump
against my naked limbs, that bristles like a hedgehog of ivory.
If I take breath again, it is only to climb
the slope where from the saddle of a rock spur
I see under the porch of my hand, guided by
fetid effluvia, like six sapless trees, white-haired
gorgons against a fog of fire, etching their twin
profiles into the bodies of tubers: they are
Egyptian mummies of these caves, dressed in their
own shadows, in silvery mist, their hands waving.
Some dark fury has driven you wild, you slobbering
Medusas, so you throw sprays of madness against the wind!
And I, who was kept so pure by the laughter of childhood
once, I was a proud boy, nothing could bend me,
but they have stolen my freedom to draw me into
their lair, if I close my eyes it is always
their voices I hear, and the bitter wish to damage me
is there in the sweetness of their invitations.
Understand, my own slim glory is extinct now, yet
this uncouth citadel was once the only theatre
of my passion, I suffer now in memory which is
my last possession, as I look within it for
any mark the child I was might have left.

RAINER MARIA RILKE

Passion

1

She lay, and let her childish arms be bound
by servants round the dried up body of the king;
her limbs spread on him sweetly all night long.
She found his withered flesh was frightening,

but turned her face into his beard, whenever
an owl hooted, or she heard any other
of the noises that belong to night. Terror
and desire both gathered in her.

The stars throbbed, as if they were fellow victims.
Through the bedchamber a certain smell rose,
and a curtain stirred as if giving a signal.
She tried to understand what it could mean.

She held herself against that dark old man,
with no black moment reached, throughout the night,
a virgin, over failing royal flesh,
still pure, and yet with all her soul alight.

2

All through the empty day the king had been
mulling over what he'd done, and what
missed out on, petting his dog as he brooded.
Then, in the evening, there was Abishag
arching over him. And suddenly the whole mess
of his past had to be laid aside, so he could sail
that dangerous sea-coast, lying beneath
the twin stars of her silent breasts.

Once an experienced lover of women,
he recognised her unkissed mouth was
unmoved, and that the inner being between
the fork of her flesh felt no desire for him.
He shivered, as he tried to summon up his
last blood, nevertheless, like a dog on a command.

ALEXANDER PUSHKIN

A Former Lover

Beneath the blue skies of her own country
    she grew sick and withered …
Even now, perhaps, somewhere above me
    her young ghost still hovers,
while I am numb, and this final separation
    rouses no more pain in me
than in the lips that, just now, calmly
    gave the news of her death.

Yet she was someone I once loved with passion,
    and all the usual anxieties:
tension, tenderness, unhappiness
    reaching almost to madness;
where has all that torment disappeared? Sadly,
    for her too trusting spirit, see,
all the sweet memory of days gone by stirs
    neither a tear nor reproach in me.

Aglaya

One man I know had my Aglaya
For his moustache and uniform.
Money won her for another.
Any Frenchman roused her warmth.
Cleon's mind excited her.
And Damis with his tender song.
Tell me, though, my dear Aglaya.
How did your spouse win your desire?

Exegi Monumentum

I've set up for myself a monument, though not in stone.
No hands have made it, and no weeds will grow
Along the path to where the stubborn
    Head soars above Alexander's column.

I shall not die altogether. Lyrics of mine,
Although my flesh decays, will hold my spirit
And I'll be known as long as any poet
    Remains alive under the moon.

News of me then will cross the whole of Russia
And every tribe there will have heard my name:
The Slavs, the Finns, and those in the wild Tungus,
    The Kalmucks on the plain.

And they will all love me, because my songs
Evoked some kindness in a cruel age,
Since I once begged for mercy to assuage
    The wrongs of the downfallen.

So, Muse, obey God's orders without fear,
Forget insults, expect no laurel wreaths;
Treat praise and slander with indifference.
    And never argue with a fool.

Index of First Lines

Dissolute, undressed, indoors, we argue 146
Distance: versts, miles ... 280
Do not look backward, children. 93
Do you think of her, geranium Yelabuga? 345
Dried up old cactus 81

Estonian ghosts of 34
Even in May now with so many yellows: 84
Even the sad music from the card radio is glamorous 185

Flew South, still drugged with white sunshine, 149
For all the stench of Bucharest car exhaust 158
For beauties delicate as twigs 13
For lovely Allen   I saw you dancing 48
For how many years along this street of mine have I 334
For the baiting 18
Forget us, children. Our conscience 287
Forgive me   bright sons   if I have hobbled 36
Forgotten, shabby and long time abandoned 94
Free day   unmarked   open 40
From the lattice bridge on Thursday a woman 29

God help us   Smoke! 238
going north: back through the 38
Going to buy milk from the corner shop 156
Grey and dingy house in Meudon, 312

Hamelin, the good-mannered 280
Here is a ring that isn't worth much money. 130
Here on the far side of Whale island 148
Here on the terrace by the donkey path 159
He's made a fire to warm him 131
High above cross and trumpet 236
His eyelids are dark as coffee, the Southerner, 316
His kiss a bristling 24
his syllables 14
Homesickness! that long 288
Hope cheers the farmer when the sky is red. 131
How marvellously you squandered yourself, 150
How can we make friends before one of us dies 184
How is your life with the other one, 278
How often 350
How readily now do I forgive you 52
However the hot grey streets are still lit 37

I know the truth – give up all other truths! 210
'I may be timid, but I am never humble,' she said. 143
I must be ill, of course. I've been shivering 326
I opened my veins.   Unstoppably 289

Lais, courtesan of Corinth, why has 73
Last night she ran out barefoot over 116
Later the cleaners come 16
Let us consider the dance between fig and wasp, 157
Little mushroom, white Bolitus, 233
Lived for 3 days on 47
London in August, watching 158
Long distance calls 347
Look at how delicate and frail I am! 130
Looking at figures of flicked ink 194

mad girl do you still 6
Marina, how I love to know that 325
Massive, heavy, with a small Kepi 315
Midnight cold of oxygen 321
Mirror, mirror, what's going on? 165
Most things I worry over never happen. 189
Much too happy always 315
Muse of lament, you are the most beautiful of 225
My answer would have to be music 72
My desk, most loyal friend 294
My ear attends to you, 248
My golden-eyed and tender-hearted son, 154
My legs shimmer like fish 49
My lips are salt, and my eyelashes. 310
My man is lost. 105
My mother wore tweed suits and court shoes. 161
My twenty-six year old ensign, 311

No one has taken anything away – 214
Nobler, they wrote on the 42
Not to defend 48
Now down George Street a 53
Now on three sides the darkness grows deeper 332
Now people say we ought to curb our appetite – 197
Now the grey light from the garden falls 45
Now we'll go homeward 323

Old aunt your 10
Old nag I 11
On a balcony in California 87
On both sides of the gardens the tall 141
On hot nights now, in the smell of trees and water 143
Once 69
Once again they've quarrelled on a tram, 311
Once in a dream a graph was already 70
Once, level with the sycamore in 44
Once or twice your nightmare 6
Once you gave me New York. 152

One man I know had my Aglaya 355
Onion on the piano under the music 35

Pink and shining as a scatter of lentils 71
Precocious, gifted girl, my nineteenth-century 156
Prince, let's have no more disturbing 238

Rain in the beech trees at 4 a.m.: 188
Rain, night, a broken window 348
Remember Melusine 57
Roy, I'm fussed by festschrifts. 190

Salt in the notch of my 34
Sealed in rainlight one 29
Shading in white streetlight on 36
Shall I fear for you as the 50
shaving in the afternoon 15
She calls *Too late* from her bed, and in fury 186
She lay, and let her childish arms be bound 353
she who has no love for women 3
Sing me a lullaby, rcok me 351
Slow and easy, in a river of black water 53
smiles and sings, in 50
Some ancestor of mine was a violinist 212
Some people treat my best gifts with suspicion 132
Stood there since World War I 39
Streets smelling of vinegar, fronted with pink 47
Strong doesn't mate with strong. 249
Sunlight on the canal, seagulls and a few boats 138
Suppose I took out a slender ketch from 27

Tell me your gods, to 46
Ten years ago, beneath the Hotel Astoria, 115
That April, even though the trees were grey 93
That whole wet summer, I listened to Louis Armstrong. 192
The air is rising tonight and the leaf dust is 73
The bed of a railway cutting 246
The bell in the hollow chapel 324
The birds are returning in May, the curlews and sandpipers, 147
The bus jumped, like a brazen 297
The chestnut trees are massed 16
The cold that killed Patel 74
The day opens, bland 99
The dead are strong. 106
The diesel stops. It is morning. Grey sky 31
The first surprise: I like it. 122
The flame of kerosene flickers. 308
The gaunt lady of the service wash 115
The house is sick. When I come down 43

The last days of October were dark and wet. 199
The leaves of four droopy tomato plants 154
The light is sullen today, yet people are 120
The moon woke me, the pocked and chalky moon 140
The present holder of the papers sits 75
the shelter,   the old washhouse 51
The shop windows of the city glitter daily 131
The Singleton is fiercer than the rest. 189
The summer garden breathes through my 155
The tram grinds on 14
The windows are black tonight. The lamp 166
The wood trade in his hands 3
There are clowds – about us 218
There are owls in the garden and a dog barking. 146
There are spores at work in the stone here, corded 83
There they all are on the lawn 118
There's a whir of wood pigeons this morning: 145
These yellow afternoons, dark skies, wet streets. 117
They shall be black metal and borne now those 67
They took   quickly, they took   hugely, 303
This is the landscape of the Cambrian age: 82
This public box is 49
'Those black eyed children begging in Bucharest 196
Through yellow fingers smoke rises about you 46
Through your erotic landscape lit with tallow flares 66
Time to return, and my fere it is carries me to the 352
To lie at the edge of the forest 318
To live here, grace 19
To see your sadness 7
To slash, split, open or break. 198
Today or tomorrow the snow will melt. 217
Today the plump flesh of a white crocus 124
Tonight   a November fever   white 45
Tonight I think this landscape could 79
Tonight our bodies lie unused like clothes flung 122
Toothless and twenty-three, fine 33
Tough as canvas, Marina, your soul 123
Two silver ghosts we cast up 41

Uncurtained, my long room floats on 63
Under hot white skies, if we could, 70

Waking cold   a squeeze of fear   the 42
Walking through so many wards to look for you 160
Water black water at night the Rhine and 64
We are keeping an eye on the girls, so that the *kvass* 214
We like to eat looking at boats. At night 162
We shall not escape Hell, my passionate 211
We speak a different language, 347

Index of Titles